W9-BVB-870

Praise for *The Making of a Democratic Economy*

"Kelly and Howard offer the insight that our democratic principles and our economic vitality don't need to be in constant contradiction. For the future health of our planet and its citizens, we need to democratize our market-driven economy by creating ownership structures that, by their very nature, lead to more sustainable, generative outcomes. This powerful book shines a light on the practical paths so many are searching for today."

—Dan Wolf, CEO, Cape Air, and former Massachusetts State Senator

"We call *The Laura Flanders Show* the place where 'the people who say it can't be done take a backseat to the people who are doing it.' Howard and Kelly bring us dispatches from places like that all across the United States, where people are democratizing the economy and shifting power. This important survey, from two who have been instrumental to much of this work, paints a picture not simply of a mosaic of experiments but of a newly emerging system that lies within our reach. Can we change our culture to cherish people over capital? It won't be easy, but it can be done. We need deep long-term thinking and immediate action steps. Lucky for us, this deeply considered book offers both."

—Laura Flanders, Host and Executive Producer, *The Laura Flanders Show*

"Marjorie Kelly and Ted Howard remind us that it's not enough to fight against an unjust and unsustainable system—we also have to have a vision for the system we want instead and a plan for building it. The stories they tell in *The Making of a Democratic Economy* lift up the hard and vital work of the people creating the institutions of the next economy."

—Kat Taylor, cofounder and CEO, Beneficial State Bank

"As champions of worker and community ownership, Kelly and Howard remind us that economic democracy is essential to political democracy and a viable human future."

—David Korten, author of *When Corporations Rule the World* and *Change the Story, Change the Future*

"This book offers a practical path of radical hope for system change. Models like those here are being copied across the world. Scores of the ideas here make clear sense, like having the Federal Reserve bail out the planet the same way it bailed out the big banks. If you're looking for a mix of mind-expanding vision with ideas and models that are working and ready to be tried in your town, this book is for you."

—Kevin Jones, cofounder of Social Capital Markets and The Transform Series

"This is an important book. It builds on growing recognition that systemic transformation is needed, providing a road map to understanding that democracy is at the core of building flourishing economies needed for a flourishing future. We all need to deeply learn from the many examples and lessons of this book and work together to create whole systems change. *The Making of a Democratic Economy* provides an invaluable guide to how that can happen."

—Sandra Waddock, Galligan Chair of Strategy, Professor of Management, Boston College

"Marjorie Kelly—a huge influence for me as an impact investor and activist—has given us another gem, on the critical need for democracy not just in our political system but in our economy."

—Morgan Simon, Founding Partner, Candide Group, and author of *Real Impact*

"The call for an economy that works for all is heard in Washington and even on Wall Street—but how will the change take place? Marjorie and Ted offer a map. They share stories of a different kind of enterprise—one that puts the human interest at the heart of success. These community-based enterprises are not only hopeful but replicable—they illuminate the design for an economy that honors our democratic ideals."

—Judith Samuelson, Executive Director, Business and Society Program, The Aspen Institute

"Marjorie Kelly and Ted Howard have given us the road map toward economic democracy. But they don't just show the interstates and the major landmarks—they show the byways and small towns where real change comes from. In this moment when greater and greater numbers of people are realizing that the rules of capitalism must be rewritten, the stories in these pages, and the strategies that Kelly and Howard share, will guide our way forward."

—Lenore Palladino, Assistant Professor of Economics and Public Policy, University of Massachusetts Amherst; former Vice President for Policy & Campaigns, Demos; and former Campaign Director, MoveOn.org

THE MAKING OF A DEMOCRATIC ECONOMY

THE MAKING OF A DEMOCRATIC ECONOMY

Building Prosperity for the Many, Not Just the Few

MARJORIE KELLY and **TED HOWARD** of
the **DEMOCRACY COLLABORATIVE**

Berrett–Koehler Publishers, Inc.

Berrett-Koehler Publishers, Inc.
1333 Broadway, Suite 1000
Oakland, CA 94612-1921
Tel: (510) 817-2277
Fax: (510) 817-2278
www.bkconnection.com

ORDERING INFORMATION
Quantity sales. Special discounts are available on quantity purchases by corporations, associations, and others. For details, contact the "Special Sales Department" at the Berrett-Koehler address above.

Individual sales. Berrett-Koehler publications are available through most bookstores. They can also be ordered directly from Berrett-Koehler: Tel: (800) 929-2929; Fax: (802) 864-7626; www.bkconnection.com.

Orders for college textbook/course adoption use. Please contact Berrett-Koehler:
Tel: (800) 929-2929; Fax: (802) 864-7626.

Distributed to the U.S. trade and internationally by Penguin Random House Publisher Services.

Printed in the United States of America

Berrett-Koehler books are printed on long-lasting acid-free paper. When it is available, we choose paper that has been manufactured by environmentally responsible processes. These may include using trees grown in sustainable forests, incorporating recycled paper, minimizing chlorine in bleaching, or recycling the energy produced at the paper mill.

Library of Congress Cataloging-in-Publication Data
Names: Kelly, Marjorie, 1953- author. Howard, Ted, 1950- author.
Title: The making of a democratic economy : building prosperity for the many, not just the few / Marjorie Kelly and Ted Howard of the Democracy Collaborative.
Description: First edition. | Oakland, CA : Berrett-Koehler Publishers, Inc., [2019] | Includes bibliographical references and index.
Identifiers: LCCN 2019004277 | ISBN 9781523099924 (print hardcover)
Subjects: LCSH: Sustainable development. | Equality. | Mixed economy.
Classification: LCC HC79.E5 K399 2019 | DDC 330.12/6—dc23
LC record available at https://lccn.loc.gov/2019004277

First Edition
27 26 25 24 23 22 21 20 19 10 9 8 7 6 5 4 3 2 1

Book producer and text designer: Maureen Forys, Happenstance Type-O-Rama
Jacket design: Rob Johnson, Toprotype, Inc.
Cover image (hands): © PA Images

To Gar Alperovitz

CONTENTS

FOREWORD

In moments of crisis, when the system around us stops working, cracks in our understanding appear—we come unmoored, unable to explain how the world works and indeed what our place in it is. But these gaps don't stay empty for long. Fear, dividing and turning us against each other, rushes in to fill the cracks—unless we can fill them with hope first.

Hope is what makes it possible to just say more than "no" in times of crisis. Don't get me wrong, saying "no"—to the rise of oligarchs and authoritarians around the globe, to the cages at the borders, to a rapidly accelerating climate crisis—is a moral imperative. But hope—credible hope, grounded in vision and strategy—is what turns reactive movements into transformative ones. We need to know what we are *for* as well as what we're *against*, illuminating the path forward with a clear and powerful vision of the world we want. That's what hope is—the light we throw on the future by our ability to dream together.

To be sustained, hope needs a foundation. It's not enough to imagine that another world is possible; we need to be able to picture it, experience it in miniature, feel and taste it. What Marjorie Kelly and Ted Howard do in the pages that follow is give us the concrete stories and real-world models that we need to truly believe in this new world.

These stories—of cooperatively owned workplaces; of cities committing to economic policies rooted in racial justice; of ethical finance and investing; of communities on the frontlines of crisis building the new—combine to show us that a different economy is not just a theoretical possibility, or a distant utopia, but something already under construction in the real world. To be sure, the road from our current economic system—extractive, brutal, and fundamentally unsustainable—to a system grounded in community, democracy, and justice remains uncertain, and there are no shortcuts. But the stories in these pages help us to understand that we can make this road as we walk it, starting by taking a first step together beyond isolation and despair.

In the stories Kelly and Howard tell, we see vital leadership emerging from those for whom the current system never worked—introducing us, for instance, to a new generation of Oglala Lakota leaders building a remarkable "regenerative community" out of the depths of poverty on the Pine Ridge Reservation. Those most brutalized and excluded need to be in the lead, yet that doesn't leave everyone else off the hook. Changing everything means that everyone has a role to play, so Kelly and Howard tell the stories not just of activists and grassroots leaders, but of the unlikely accomplices of the democratic economy, where the seeds of a future beyond corporate capitalism are being planted in hospital procurement departments, pension fund offices, and even a few company boardrooms. And it's not that radicals have snuck in to subvert these economic institutions—it's that the failing system all around us is making what was once radical seem more like common sense, including for those with the power to move significant resources out of the current system and into the next one.

There's a saying activists in South America use often, about making a revolution from below as *trabajo de hormigas* ("the work of the ants"). That's an apt way to understand the work of the community wealth builders Kelly and Howard explore—working below the surface, coordinated without central control, digging tunnels to what comes next.

Kelly and Howard approach all this with humility—the work of the ants is done by human beings, not superheroes or prophets; the way the authors acknowledge their own failures and missteps along the way gives us space to be OK with our own. Failure is important here because a democratic economy is a work in progress, built on and learning from experiments, some wildly successful, some not. Kelly and Howard tell us about a new economic system emerging from these experiments in the laboratories of democracy, where the hard work of inventing and testing alternatives at the local level lays the groundwork for the new institutions that can emerge at scale when the political opening presents itself. This has happened before—it's how the New Deal was built in the US, and how Canada's single-payer system came to be. Something powerful is at work, but we need to be ready to build for the long haul, committed to a lifetime of engagement.

It's fitting that the title of Kelly and Howard's book calls to mind the work of the great British historian E. P. Thompson, whose *Making of the English Working Class* insists that the working class didn't emerge from nowhere as a complete social and cultural identity, nor was it simply fashioned passively by history. Thompson, on the contrary, insists that the English working class was "present at its own making"—building itself through its own agency, its own acts of resistance, and its own ability to dream of a better world. A democratic economy, too, is present at its own making. It's not something that just hovers as an abstract possibility on the horizon, nor is it something that's going to happen automatically—it's something we need to start building, together, now.

But we need to hurry. Patience and time have run out for so many of our collective struggles. It's past time to reckon with and repair the damage done by slavery and colonialism, and it's past time to take bold action to prevent catastrophic climate change. As Kelly and Howard point out, making space to build the world we want in the face of these crises means that slow experimentation isn't enough—we need to be ready for big steps that give that new world the breathing room it needs to come into being. For instance, in the last financial crisis, our governments conjured hundreds of billions of dollars out of thin air to save the financial sector. Why can't we use that kind of power to attack the climate crisis at its extractive root, by buying out and winding down the fossil fuel companies—and by prioritizing the most marginalized communities in the transition?

If one thing is certain, it's that more crises are on their way. We know that the shock doctors of the old system are making plans to take advantage of these crises—laying the foundations for more repression, for more extraction, for more austerity, for more Flints, more Puerto Ricos, more

Brazils. We need plans and models, too. The more we build the democratic economy today, the better prepared we are to grab the wheel of history and swerve toward the next system. This book arrives just in time.

—NAOMI KLEIN, Canadian social activist, filmmaker, and author of *No Is Not Enough, This Changes Everything, The Shock Doctrine,* and *No Logo*

PREFACE

In scattered experiments—disconnected, often unaware of one another—unsung leaders are building the beginnings of what many of us hunger for but can scarcely imagine is possible: an economy that might enable us all to live well, and to do so within planetary boundaries. They're laying pathways toward an economy of, by, and for the people. Visiting these leaders, we have distilled the first principles at work. What we find emerging is a coherent paradigm for how to organize an economy—one that takes us beyond the binary choice of corporate capitalism versus state socialism into something new.

The first moral principles of this system are community and sustainability, for as indigenous peoples have long known, the two are one and the same. Other principles are creating opportunity for those long excluded, and putting labor before capital; ensuring that assets are broadly held, and that investing is for people and place, with profit the result, not the primary aim; designing enterprises for a new era of equity and sustainability; and evolving ownership beyond a primitive notion of maximum extraction to an advanced concept of stewardship.

This emerging democratic economy is in stark contrast to today's extractive economy, designed for financial extraction by an elite. It's an economy of, by, and for the 1 percent. Society long ago democratized government, but we have never democratized the economy. That is the historical project now beginning. There's a role for all of us in nourishing this potential next system.

This book is for all who are concerned about the fate of our planet and civilization. It can be of value to activists and to those from both sides of the political aisle who recognize the status quo isn't sustainable. It will be useful for leaders from foundations, nonprofit hospital systems, colleges and universities, government and nonprofit economic development, impact investing, progressive and employee-owned companies, unions, mayors, and other civic leaders. Political scientists and economists may find it of value, though it's not an academic book.

These readers are international. The stories here are predominantly from the US and UK, the epicenter and birthplace of capitalism. But the lessons apply in many nations, for the extractive economy is global, and the democratic economy is likewise rising across the world. Each chapter visits one site where this work is emerging; feel free to jump directly to the chapter that interests you most.

The two of us, coauthors Marjorie Kelly and Ted Howard, are executives at The Democracy Collaborative, a 19-year-old nonprofit that is a research and development lab for a democratic economy. Our staff of 40 plus a dozen fellows—in Washington, DC, Cleveland, Ohio, Brussels, Belgium, Preston, England, and elsewhere—work in theory and practice to incubate ideas for transformative economic change. We work at the level of systems creating the crises making the headlines. In our place-based work, we help communities create wealth that stays local and is broadly shared, through economic development fed by the power of anchor institutions, built on locally rooted ownership. In our theory, research, and policy work, we envision large-scale system change in areas such as the environment, finance, and ownership design.

In recent years, our staff has tripled as demand for our services has grown. This growth has occurred because of a rising thirst for transformative solutions, and because of a group of visionary funders who share that thirst. We've reached the point where we cannot work with every community, organization, or political leader seeking our partnership. That led us to write this book, to open-source what we and many others have learned.

This book is the work of two minds writing as one, so you'll find us speaking of each other in third person—"Marjorie" and "Ted." Marjorie

Kelly, executive vice president at The Democracy Collaborative and lead author, brings long experience with progressive business and investing as a journalist, cofounder and president of *Business Ethics* magazine, author of two previous books, and hands-on designer of company and financial architectures for social mission and broad ownership. Ted Howard, president and cofounder of The Democracy Collaborative, helped the Cleveland Foundation and others design and develop the employee-owned Evergreen Cooperatives and works widely with anchor institutions such as nonprofit hospital systems, colleges, and universities and, increasingly, with political leaders on both sides of the Atlantic.

We're radicals with our feet on the ground. This book is intended to help the reader see that a new system is in the making. In the different models, approaches, and ideologies we encounter in our visits, we see a coherent, new system paradigm in formation. We hope you come away understanding this potential path forward and how you can join others in walking it.

INTRODUCTION
FROM CLEVELAND TO PRESTON

A new paradigm for economic transformation

There can be no real political democracy unless there is something approaching an economic democracy.

—THEODORE ROOSEVELT

Where there is no vision, the people perish.

—PROVERBS 29:18

Imagine, for a moment, a business owner positioned to benefit from the next big thing in our economy, the person emblematic of the innovation that will transform the economy. Picture that owner this way: an African-American man, early 40s, formerly incarcerated, at one time a drug dealer, employed at a commercial laundry.

His name is Chris Brown. He sold crack cocaine more than 20 years ago in the Cleveland neighborhood of Glenville, an unlikely place to find the seeds of the next political economy growing.

Cleveland is the city Rockefeller built. John D. Rockefeller made Cleveland the home of Standard Oil, and the city in its heyday had more headquarters of Fortune 500 firms than any place but New York. Steelworkers in Cleveland, highly organized by unions, once made the highest hourly wages in the nation. With that prosperity came the mansions of Glenville and the elegant sculpture gardens and manicured lawns of nearby Rockefeller Park.

Today, Cleveland is the city Rockefeller abandoned. The flight of white residents and businesses grew in the 1960s, cutting the city's population by more than half from its 1950s peak. Once one of America's wealthiest large cities, it is now one of its poorest. And Glenville, now 95 percent black, is one of Cleveland's poorest neighborhoods. On Glenville's South Boulevard, a once-stately three-story brick home sold a few years back for $5,000.

That's the neighborhood Chris came home to after three years in prison. He faced long odds against making a good living there, with unemployment at 24 percent and median annual income around $19,000. Back in 1993, Chris was attending college and had dreams for himself. But his girlfriend became pregnant and he had to drop out. With no marketable skills and a new baby to feed, he turned to selling drugs.

After serving his time, Chris found work as a roofer, at a telemarketing company, and as a janitor, all at low pay with no benefits.[1] *Then he landed a spot with Evergreen Cooperative Laundry.*

The laundry is one of three Evergreen Cooperatives—the other two are a green energy company, Evergreen Energy Solutions, and Green City Growers, an urban vegetable farm—employing 212 people in all. They're owned by their workers, and each worker gets one share and one vote. Their mission includes hiring people like Chris and other formerly incarcerated residents of Cleveland's deteriorating neighborhoods. Their customers include large, local nonprofits, such as the Cleveland Clinic, that remained rooted in these neighborhoods as other businesses and institutions left. These are considered *anchor institutions* because they're anchored in place, not inclined to abandon their community as profit-maximizing corporations did. These anchors are being harnessed to buy goods and services from local businesses that hire, train, and empower local residents, thus recycling wealth in the community, in contrast to absentee corporations that draw wealth out of the community.

At Evergreen, Chris started at $10 an hour with benefits, a living wage in Cleveland's economy at that time. Within six months, he became plant supervisor, with a raise. Most importantly, Chris got a piece of ownership, sharing in the decision-making and in the fruit of those decisions.

Chris's story is at the center of a flourishing venture known as the Cleveland Model. It's a new approach to economic development. But it's far more. It's a demonstration project for a new, democratic economy—emerging from the wreckage of the old—that is designed to serve the many, not just the few.

AN ECONOMY OF, BY, AND FOR THE PEOPLE

A *democratic economy* is an economy of the people, by the people, and for the people. It's an economy that, in its fundamental design, aims to meet the essential needs of all of us, balance human consumption with the regenerative capacity of the earth, respond to the voices and concerns of regular people, and share prosperity without regard to race, gender, national origin, or wealth. At the core of a democratic economy is the common good, in keeping with the founding aims of democracy in politics. "There must be a positive passion for the public good, the public interest," as John Adams wrote, "and this public passion must be superior to all private passions."[2]

A democratic economy designs social architectures around what we value, with community and sustainability the alpha and omega, our interrelatedness and interdependence at the center. It involves the development of what ecologists call *symbioses*. As conservationist Aldo Leopold once put it, "Politics and economics are advanced symbioses" in which free-for-all competition is replaced by structures for cooperation.[3]

That's not to say a democratic economy is a utopia in which all our problems will be solved. What it does mean is that it's possible to design ordinary economic activity to serve broad well-being, not to extract maximum profits.

The system of democracy produced by the American Revolution is rightfully criticized for its deep and tragic flaws—most flagrantly, slavery, but also denial of citizenship rights to people of color, women, and those without property. Yet the founders fed a revolutionary river that flowed far beyond their limitations, working a radical transformation in society, which for millennia across the globe had been designed to serve the elite of the monarchy and aristocracy. The new system of democracy, as historian Gordon S. Wood observed, "made the interests and prosperity of ordinary people—their pursuit of happiness—the goal."[4]

Yet this new system democratized only government, not the economy. A democratic economy is about completing in the economic realm the work begun by the founders in the political realm. The movement for a democratic economy forms a tributary to many streams of liberation flowing through history, from abolition and women's suffrage to the formation of unions and the rights of gay marriage. As *New York Times* columnist Michelle Alexander wrote, "the revolutionary river that brought us this far just might be the only thing that can carry us to a place where we all belong."[5]

AN ECONOMY OF, BY, AND FOR THE 1 PERCENT

When the US Constitution was written, the Industrial Revolution, engineered by the new aristocracy of the railroad barons and kings of capital, had not yet emerged. The word *corporation* appears nowhere in that document. But by 1813 John Adams was writing to Thomas Jefferson, "Aristocracy, like Waterfowl, dives for ages and then rises with brighter plumage."[6]

We've seen that happen throughout American history, from the Gilded Age of the late 19th century to the "new Gilded Age" of the 21st. Today we live in a world in which 26 billionaires own as much wealth as half the planet's population.[7] The three wealthiest men in the US—Bill Gates, Jeff

Bezos, and Warren Buffett—own more wealth than the bottom half of America combined, a total of 160 million people.[8] Since 2009, 95 percent of income gains in the US have gone to the top 1 percent.[9] Meanwhile, an alarming 47 percent of Americans cannot put together even $400 in the face of an emergency, leaving most of us unprepared to face such ordinary mishaps as a flat tire or a child's twisted ankle.[10]

Our economy is not only failing the vast majority of our people, it is literally destroying our planet. It's consuming natural resources at more than one-and-a-half times the earth's ability to regenerate them.[11] Soil depletion has ravaged one-third of all arable land.[12] Nearly two-thirds of all vertebrates have disappeared from the earth since 1970, part of a sixth mass extinction that is terrifyingly underway.[13] We are razing the only home our civilization has, yet we remain caught inside a system designed to perpetuate that razing, in order to feed wealth to an elite.

Ours is an economy "Of the 1%, By the 1%, For the 1%," as economist Joseph Stiglitz put it.[14] At its core, it has what we, the coauthors, call *capital bias*, a favoritism toward finance and wealth-holders that is woven invisibly throughout the system. We might call it an *extractive economy*, for it's designed to enable a financial elite to extract maximum gain for themselves, everywhere on the globe, heedless of damage created for workers, communities, and the environment.

Capital bias is often advanced by policy—as with lower taxes on capital gains than on labor income, bailouts for big banks but not for ordinary homeowners, or tax breaks given to large corporations that put small locally owned companies out of business. Yet capital bias also lies more deeply in basic economic architectures and norms, in institutions and asset ownership. Speculative investors holding stock shares for minutes enjoy the rights of owners, while employees working at a corporation for decades are dispossessed, lacking a claim on the profits they help to create.

We're all caught in this system. Pointing fingers won't change it. But we need to get it—really get it in our gut—that the design of the extractive economy lies behind today's multiplying crises. We can see this in the way the financial elite wields its wealth to overpower democracy, the way wages are held down and jobs automated out of existence, the way the growth mandate overpowers the planet's resilience.

IN THE BELLY OF THE BEAST

Using old approaches to regulate this system is like putting a picket fence in front of a bulldozer. Take the minimum wage. Certainly a higher minimum wage is vitally needed. But it's a solution from last century, when more people had full-time jobs at single employers. Today, 40 percent of jobs in the US are insecure, part-time, contract, gig-economy–type work, and even those jobs are disappearing in the face of offshoring and automation.[15] We're getting these precarious jobs because of the system's natural functioning. The reality is that the pursuit of profits often means holding down wages—and that's a feature, not a bug. In fact, we haven't fully confronted the fact that corporations believe they have a *fiduciary duty* to systematically suppress labor and labor income—and weaken environmental regulation—in order to increase profit for wealthy shareholders.

But that confrontation is starting, with an eye toward building a more democratic economy.

Senator Elizabeth Warren's Accountable Capitalism Act is an example. She proposes that all corporations with more than $1 billion in revenue be required to obtain new federal corporate charters with broader fiduciary duties. Overnight, large corporations would have a new internal purpose: they'd be required to consider the interests of workers and communities, in addition to stockholders. Workers would get seats on boards.[16]

Similarly radical is the Labour Party plan in the United Kingdom for inclusive ownership funds (IOFs). This proposed legislation would require companies with 250 or more employees to transfer 1 percent of ownership into an IOF each year, until the funds hold at least 10 percent ownership of each firm. The funds would be run by worker trustees, wielding the substantial clout of voting rights. And workers would receive dividends—a slice of profits—just as all shareholders do.[17]

There's the Green New Deal advanced by US Congresswoman Alexandria Ocasio-Cortez. Not only would this plan for a massive public works program to shift to 100 percent renewable energy in 10 years create tens of thousands—possibly millions—of jobs, but it would also open up possibilities for system-level policy changes to advance shared prosperity as well as sustainability.

Or consider the problem of the big banks. After the 2008 financial crisis, the big financial players who caused the crisis got bailed out, allowing them to return to mischief as usual. A more radical movement in the US and UK is pushing for publicly owned banks, like the Bank of North Dakota, owned by the state, with assets of more than $7 billion, which helped that state avoid the ravages of the downturn. Banks rooted in community are already in place across Germany. Now community leaders and elected officials from London to Los Angeles are exploring the idea. New Jersey Governor Phil Murphy, a former Wall Street banker, is committed to establishing a state public bank, as is Gavin Newsome, the new governor of California.[18]

These kinds of policies begin to get to the core of the system. They get beyond tax-and-spend transfer measures, which today are being dismantled by tax cuts and austerity. They get beyond the regulatory state, today being crushed beneath the onslaught of deregulation, privatization, and the dismantling of government. These new approaches don't seek to simply put back what's being destroyed. They point to how a whole new system is being born now, in the belly of the beast. They herald a potentially profound shift from an extractive economy to a democratic economy.

The problem is that people by and large don't see this—not even the people who are part of it. The work of employee-owned companies, impact investing, public banking, racial justice in economic development, local purchasing by anchor institutions, and more is being done in siloed activities all over the world. But it's a movement that doesn't know it's a movement.

TOO MANY NAMES

It's not that the new system hasn't been named. It has too many names: *stakeholder capitalism*, the *solidarity economy*, *new economy*, *sharing economy*, *regenerative economy*, the *living economy*. Some call themselves impact investors, others, mission investors. Some work passionately for worker cooperatives, while others support employee stock ownership plans (ESOPs), and sometimes the two groups take potshots at each other.

A new generation of progressives and visionary political leaders have embraced the label *socialist,* and certainly their emergence is an explosive development for positive change. Yet the use of this term begs the question: Why do we feel constrained by a supposed binary choice between capitalism and socialism?

The struggle for new language is a sign of the times. We stand at a turning point where many share a sense of peril about the possibility of systemic collapse, "a heightened sense that civilizations are themselves vulnerable," philosopher Jonathan Lear writes. At such a time of radical cultural disruption, he says, history holds out to us a "call for concepts." As the old system fails, we're losing the conceptual world that has given our lives meaning. To move into the new, we need the skill of "imaginative excellence." We need sweepingly new vision and new naming.[19]

State socialism isn't it. Corporate capitalism isn't it. An economy adequate to today's challenges just isn't there in those 19th-century paradigms. The *democratic economy* isn't yet a term in common use. It's offered here as a unifying frame for the movement that doesn't know it's a movement, helping more of us recognize the potential for system-level transformation, to be unafraid of real ambition.

A democratic economy isn't a top-down command economy. It isn't capitalism plus more regulations and social safety nets, nor is it capitalism plus green technologies. Building a democratic economy is about redesigning basic institutions and activities—companies, investments, economic development, employment, purchasing, banking, resource use—so that the core functioning of the economy is designed to serve the common good. Anything less than deep redesign will likely fail to see us through the tumultuous era ahead for the earth community.

BEYOND BARNACLES ON THE WHALE

Democracy needs to move *inside the economy*. Putting such values as sustainability or fairness on the outside of the system through regulation and social safety nets is like attaching barnacles to the side of a whale. These values need to be in the DNA.

The soul of a new system is its first principles. These are what knit together diverse approaches into a common paradigm. Systems thinking tells us human systems are self-organized around what we naturally care about, our values. Self-organization also means that, when old ways stop working, systems have the capacity "to change themselves utterly by creating whole new structures and behaviors," as systems theorist Donella Meadows wrote. That's what is underway, spontaneously, in our time.[20]

The first principle of the old system is capital bias; that's at the core of the capital-ist system that serves the interests of the wealthy few. Serving the common good is the core of the new system. This plays out through seven principles of a democratic economy, which we find organically embraced by the people we visit in this book. They are principles of *community, inclusion, place, good work, democratic ownership, sustainability,* and *ethical finance.* These represent a new common sense.

In chapter 1, we look at how they contrast with the principles of the extractive economy, as we also look at the surprising, largely invisible worldwide phenomenon of the democratic economy quietly arising. In each subsequent chapter, we take up one principle, as seen in the work of some remarkable folks.

In chapter 2, we visit Nick Tilsen, a thirty-something Lakota Sioux on Pine Ridge Indian Reservation in South Dakota, who has begun building a regenerative community that will produce all its own energy, while training youth in construction skills and creating an employee-owned construction company and Native women's quilting cooperative. The *principle of community*—where the common good comes first—is at the core of the indigenous worldview. It's a different mindset from that of high-tech founders seeking to become billionaires even as one out of three children in Silicon Valley faces hunger throughout the year.[21]

In chapter 3, we visit Tyrone Poole, a young, formerly homeless African-American who became entrepreneur of the year in Oregon, and who was aided by the city economic development organization that renamed itself Prosper Portland as part of its focus on racial justice and gender equality. The *principle of inclusion* is at work, creating opportunity for those long excluded. It begins by acknowledging—as leaders of Prosper Portland did—that the present economic system has been built on a foundation of racial exclusion and dispossession.

In chapter 4, we meet Kim Shelnik, vice president of human resources at University Hospitals in Cleveland, who is creating innovative ways to train and hire locally from the disadvantaged neighborhoods at the hospital's doorstep. What motivates anchor institutions like these is the *principle of place*—a shared devotion to a particular place, as they seek to build community wealth that stays local. This contrasts with our globalized economy's indifference to place, where corporations view places primarily as either better or worse for financial extraction.

In chapter 5, we talk with the leaders of Cooperative Home Care Associates (CHCA) in the Bronx, an employee-owned company employing 2,300 mostly Latina and African-American women. This company is built on the *principle of good work*, with labor coming before capital. CHCA is an island of human decency amid an extractive economy increasingly hostile to worker prosperity.

Chapter 6 brings us Loren Jensen, the ecological scientist who founded EA Engineering, an environmental consulting firm with 500 employees and revenue of $140 million. For a time, this firm's shares traded on NASDAQ. Under pressure for short-term profit maximization, the company cycled through three presidents, saw morale collapse, and ended up in trouble with the Securities and Exchange Commission. Loren bought it back, and it is now an employee-owned for-benefit corporation, with a commitment to the public good in its governing frame. It's a model of enterprise design for an era of equity and sustainability, embodying the *principle of democratic ownership*. It shows a potential evolution beyond the extractive corporate model, where fiduciary duty to maximize returns to shareholders is believed to be the primary moral obligation.

In chapter 7, we explore the work of Carla Santos Skandier, our colleague and a young lawyer, formerly with the Rio de Janeiro Environmental Protection Agency, who is advancing an audacious idea to break the gridlock on climate change legislation: buy out the 25 largest US fossil fuel companies using the power of the Federal Reserve. Such a move is emblematic of the *principle of sustainability*, showing what it would mean to truly put sustaining life on the planet ahead of short-term financial gains.

In chapter 8, we talk with Matthew Brown, half-time city council leader in Preston, England, a town that saw its efforts to attract a large corporation shattered after the 2008 financial meltdown. Inspired by the Cleveland Model, Preston created a model that goes far beyond it, with a new credit union, a nonpredatory payday lender, and potentially a new community-owned bank. At work is the *principle of ethical finance*, where lending is for people and place—a critically needed aspect of taking our fate back from the impersonal forces of extractive finance.

Each of these places might be considered a *laboratory of democracy*—a term coined by US Supreme Court Justice Louis Brandeis, who, during the Great Depression, said states may serve as laboratories for "novel social and economic experiments without risk to the rest of the country."[22] At the onset of the Depression, farmers gathered together in cooperatives and federations to even the odds against corporate conglomerates. Alaska established a program giving aid to elderly people who lacked caregivers. City and rural leaders built publicly owned sewer, water, and electrical systems.

These kinds of initiatives formed the basis for Social Security, national agricultural investment, and the Tennessee Valley Authority. Experiments we visit in this book can likewise pave pathways to scale. Such possibilities for scale are explored throughout the chapters, with some ideas on what we all can do—and some thoughts on large questions left to tackle—in a brief conclusion.

STARVED FOR SOMETHING NEW

Most of us know that our economic system is broken; 71 percent of Americans say they believe the economic system is rigged against them.[23]

Strange to say, that breakdown isn't the real problem we confront. The system is broken, yes, but the larger challenge is that we feel terrified by the scale of the problem, and that we despair that anything can be done. The enemy to be overcome is our sense of futility, discouragement, and paralysis. Lacking a shared and practical vision of a next system, we're unable to believe such an alternative could ever be built. Many of us can more easily envision the end of the world than we can envision the end of capitalism.

People come from all over to walk through the Evergreen Cooperative Laundry—policymakers, staff members of mayors' offices, economic development leaders, investors, hospital system administrators, foundation staff. They come to see the employee-owners pushing towels and sheets into commercial washers because this place silently tells them—at least in microcosm, at least here—something new is possible. Energized by Evergreen, related models have been created in numerous places, including St. Paul; Milwaukee; Albuquerque; Rochester, New York; and Richmond, Virginia.

Preston, England, once deemed the "suicide capital of England," was inspired by Evergreen and built a more far-reaching model; in 2018 it was named by PricewaterhouseCoopers (PwC) and the London think tank Demos as the most improved city in the UK.[24] Preston has in turn inspired city leaders across England, Scotland, Wales, and as far away as Tanzania to reexamine what's possible locally. Its success has led to the creation of a community wealth building unit in the UK Labour Party. That party is headed by Jeremy Corbyn, who entered 2019 having a good shot at becoming the next prime minister. *The Economist* called Preston Corbyn's "model town."

It's not just leftists and Labour leaders who are interested. When the US Congress in 2018 passed new employee ownership legislation, it had bipartisan cosponsorship.[25] In England, Conservative leader Edward Carpenter from Rochdale is looking at how he can build community wealth in his town.[26] In the US, New Mexico Republican Richard Berry, until recently mayor of Albuquerque, was at the table when Healthy Neighborhoods Albuquerque was built, helping large anchor institutions buy locally, an initiative modeled on Cleveland.[27]

The Cleveland Model and Preston are magnetic because of how starved we are for a glimpse of what might come next. These places embody the unlikely, seemingly foolhardy trust that amid our society's growing political, economic, and ecological chaos, something good can emerge. Something is already emerging, as people join together.

✦ ✦ ✦

In Cleveland, Chris Brown's work at Evergreen put him in a position to make a leap in his career. He left the laundry for a job with a global company where he now makes $60,000 a year. Evergreen "gave me a chance when most wouldn't," he wrote to us by email. "It gave me the skills and confidence I needed to be a leader of men!"[28]

After the Evergreen Cooperative Laundry tallied annual profits not long ago, the employees enjoyed profit-sharing bonuses of about $4,000 each. Twenty-one workers have participated in an Evergreen program to help them purchase rehabilitated houses, costing $15,000 to $30,000, through payroll deductions of roughly $400 a month, plus property tax abatement by the city. Tim Coleman—once a driver for the laundry, later promoted to customer service manager—bought a four-bedroom, two-bath home in Glenville in 2014. He will own it free and clear in 2019.[29]

Through the Cleveland Model—this green shoot of a democratic economy—something has emerged that's in scarce supply these days. As Chris told reporter Dale Maharidge shortly before he left Evergreen: "What I've got that I didn't have is hope."[30]

1

AN ECONOMY OF, BY, AND FOR THE PEOPLE

THE GREAT WAVE RISING WORLDWIDE

Principles of a democratic vs. extractive economy

Like air, I'll rise.

—MAYA ANGELOU

"You can feel the tow of the tsunami," Sandy Wiggins said. "There's a great wave rising, and you can feel the power of it, even though it's just beginning."

He was speaking to two dozen of us seated in a circle with him at a San Francisco gathering of community foundations to learn about place-based impact investing, where the aim is to earn financial returns while creating social or ecological benefit. Marjorie was there as a visiting specialist in mission design for finance. Sandy—former chair of the US Green Building Council—was part of the organizing team from the Business Alliance for Local Living Economies and RSF Social Finance.[1]

It was the group's first meeting, and a foundation president asked, "What is impact investing?" It was a safe place to admit you had no clue. Yet by the end of the cohort's 18 months together, most of these community foundations—in areas from the rural South to urban Rhode Island—had launched their own place-based investing project: turning a parking lot into a high-rise, mixed-use project; starting a local investing fund; developing a large urban farm in a food desert; or persuading a board to devote 5 percent of a nearly $1 billion endowment to place-based impact investing.

As these philanthropic leaders sat together, what was striking was the fire and heart in the room. These were people stewarding hundreds of millions of dollars in assets, conspiring like college kids in a dorm plotting revolution. Then they'd go home, wrestle with cautious boards and investment advisers telling them they couldn't do these things, yet go on to make real projects happen.

The movement for a democratic economy is a different kind of revolution. It relies on the momentum of activists, grassroots leaders, and progressive politicians, but it also involves unlikely allies like these foundation leaders, as well as impact investors and progressive business leaders: innovators who are stewards of wealth. Also involved are mayors and governors, economic development leaders, and nonprofit directors. It's an unlikely stew of talent and fire and boldness.

AN INVISIBLE ARMY

Few people understand the reach of the redesign already underway. Nonprofits are running social enterprises that exist to hire the hard-to-employ, like Tech Dump in Minneapolis, which trains the formerly incarcerated in electronics recycling. Social enterprises use business methods to tackle social problems. A network of these, the Social Enterprise Alliance, has more than 900 members in 42 states.[2] Social entrepreneurship is taught at business schools like Oxford, Harvard, and Yale.

Increasing numbers of nonprofit hospital systems are working on local economic development, like Rush University Medical Center on Chicago's West side, with net assets of $1.7 billion and total operating revenue of about $2.4 billion.[3] To address entrenched poverty among communities of color there, Rush set out to use all its resources—buying, hiring, investing locally—to affect the social determinants of health, such as job scarcity, poor education, and violence. US hospitals and health systems spend more than $782 billion each year, employ 5.6 million, and have investment portfolios of $400 billion. As more, like Rush, take up the anchor mission of serving their communities, the potential for game-changing impact is substantial.[4]

Worker-owned cooperatives are growing rapidly—like Si Se Puede!, a Brooklyn house-cleaning enterprise owned primarily by Latinas. After Cristina, a Mexican immigrant and single mother, joined this cooperative, she saw her wages jump from $7 to $20 an hour.[5] Unions are launching worker cooperatives; an example is Communications Workers of America Local 7777, which incubated Green Taxi in Denver, with a leadership and board made up entirely of immigrant drivers from East Africa and Morocco.[6] Cities advancing worker co-ops include New York City; Newark, New Jersey; Oakland, California; Rochester, New York; and Madison, Wisconsin.

Companies with employee stock ownership plans (ESOPs) number more than 6,600 in the US, and ESOPs hold assets of close to $1.4 trillion.[7] Included are companies like women's clothing firm Eileen Fisher, with 1,100 employees, and New Belgium Brewing, the maker of Fat Tire Amber Ale and the fourth largest craft brewer in the country, 100 percent owned by its employees.[8]

Employee ownership is advancing in Britain, Scotland, and many other nations and includes companies like the John Lewis Partnership, the largest department store chain in the UK with 2018 revenue of £10.2 billion. The company's 85,500 employees are all partners in the business, and each has a voice in how the company is run through a democratic system that has operated for close to a century.[9]

Also embodying deep change are 5,400 benefit corporations incorporated under statutes in 34 US states, including firms like Kickstarter and King Arthur Flour, which have embraced a legal commitment to the public good. There are the 2,655 similar B Corporations in 60 countries, certified by the nonprofit B Lab.[10]

The US cooperative sector—businesses owned by the people they serve—represents more than $500 billion in revenue and employs 2 million people, yet it remains surprisingly invisible and is rarely discussed in business schools. Cooperatives include credit unions, which are member-owned; agricultural cooperatives like Sunkist, Ocean Spray, Land O' Lakes, and Organic Valley; and consumer cooperatives like REI. Worldwide, cooperatives employ more than 12.6 million and have more than 1 billion members, with combined revenues of well over $3 trillion. Among the largest is the Mondragon Corporation of Spain, a worker-owned federation including 98 worker-owned cooperatives, with 80,000 workers and €12 billion in revenue. It sells products worldwide and has its own bank, university, business incubators, and social welfare agency.[11]

The so-called "social economy" is substantial in Canada, particularly in Quebec, which has more than 7,000 collective businesses with annual revenue of more than $40 billion. Quebec has committed as much as $100 million in some years to advance the sector, and Canada's federal government created a cocreation steering group of people from across the nation to help develop its social economy strategy.[12]

Public ownership has begun to reemerge across the world as a viable strategy in the wake of the 2008 financial crisis. Beginning in Latin America, there's been a global movement to reclaim community ownership of water systems after the disastrous failure of many extractive, investor-owned water ventures. This movement has reclaimed public ownership of water in at least 235 cases in 37 countries, benefiting 100 million people.[13] In the UK, the tides of public opinion have turned dramatically against the privatization led by Prime Minister Margaret Thatcher. In a 2017 poll, the free market think tank Legatum Institute, to its horror, found overwhelming public support for nationalizing various industries:

83 percent supported public ownership of water, 77 percent gas and electricity, 76 percent trains, 66 percent defense and aerospace, and 50 percent banks. "Written off for so long as a relic of the past," our colleague Thomas Hanna has written, "public ownership may again be taking its rightful place" among strategies for creating a better future.[14]

State-owned banks already play significant roles in places like India, China, Germany, and Latin America, and in many cases, helped those nations survive the Great Recession of 2008. In the European Union, there are more than 200 public and semipublic banks, with another 80-plus funding agencies, comprising about 20 percent of all bank assets. Germany's 413 publicly owned municipal savings banks, Sparkassen, hold more than €1.2 trillion in assets. And, as *The Economist* noted, these banks came through the global financial crisis "with barely a scratch."[15]

In another model, more than 1,100 community development financial institutions exist in the US, financed to a large extent by investors.[16] They are part of an impact investing field growing rapidly across the globe. A 2016 survey by the Global Impact Investing Network (GIIN) found impact investors had committed $22.1 billion into some 8,000 investments, out of the portfolios of investors who collectively manage close to $114 billion in assets. GIIN cofounder and CEO Amit Bouri predicts "Impact investing will become part of 'a new normal,' galvanizing capital markets to play a significant role in tackling or even solving big global challenges such as poverty, inequality, and environmental degradation."[17]

It adds up to a force bigger than most anyone knows. Our society is in a moment of breakdown, yet we're also in a time of deep redesign. That's the source of aliveness we see so often in the communities we visit and work in. There's a feeling of something frozen beginning to flow, the paralysis of fear or despondency or confusion ("What is impact investing?") becoming forward motion.

WHY BRING DEMOCRACY INTO THE ECONOMY?

Democracy provides a unifying concept for this work. The reason was articulated well by philosopher John Dewey. He said democracy is not "simply and solely a form of government," but is an ethical ideal, relevant to many social spheres, including the economy and the workplace. In Dewey's view, the ability to be a mature moral actor, to experience freedom and human dignity, best comes to fruition when we live and work inside the welcoming, human-scale, ethical design of democratic social institutions of many kinds.[18]

Dewey's thought prefigured that of Amartya Sen, the Nobel Prize–winning economist, who described economic development as a process of removing "various types of unfreedoms"—such as poverty and lack of economic opportunity—"that leave people with little choice." Sen contrasted this with narrower measures of development, such as gross domestic product (GDP) growth or technological advance. What Dewey and Sen hold out is a vision of freedom achievable only in a democratic economy: not the freedom of corporations to roam the globe in search of maximum financial extraction, but real economic prosperity for all.[19]

By contrast, the extractive economy is about the privilege of the few. The capital bias at its core is rooted in the human heart, in the perpetual quest for status. This value system is given expression through institutions, processes, and policies favoring those who possess wealth. Values and institutions combine to create an unequal distribution of privileges, resources, and power between the owners of capital and everyone else.[20]

Bias based on wealth is as illegitimate as bias based on race or sex. Yet although racism and sexism are far from eradicated in society, each has at least lost widespread legitimacy. The same cannot be said of this third form of bias, capital-ism.

Another word for capital is *assets*. Owning and controlling assets is the defining characteristic of virtually every economy, as The Democracy Collaborative cofounder and political economist Gar Alperovitz has often observed. In the ancient monarchy, the king and aristocracy owned the land of the agrarian society. In communism, the state owns the means of production. In early-stage capitalism, the robber barons owned the infrastructure of the rising industrial economy. In our era, ownership has passed into financial markets, which is why we now think of assets as financial numbers. That's the lens through which the extractive economy defines economic success, the lens of benefit to asset holders:

a rising stock market, maximum profits, growing returns to investment portfolios.

Systems produce outcomes, not as aberrations but as logical results of how they're constructed, what the goals are, who holds power. If we want outcomes consistent with the spirit and vision of a democratic economy, we need to design for these at the system level. The essence of any human system is its first principles.

PRINCIPLES OF THE DEMOCRATIC ECONOMY VS. THE EXTRACTIVE ECONOMY

The principle of community: *The common good comes first.* Community is the foundational principle of a democratic economy. At the base of such a system is a picture of the self as person-in-community, a concept articulated by ecological economist Herman Daly and theologian John Cobb. The self-contained individual in the real world does not exist, they write, because the social character of human life is primary. Community creates the conditions in which each of us may flourish. The ultimate community is the earth, for good lives are not possible without a healthy environmental ecosystem.[21]

By contrast, the extractive economy's picture of the self is an isolated individual—a rational economic man out to maximize his own gains, or in business, the self-made man. These concepts nourish fantasies of individual triumph that shape behavior in destructive ways, encouraging aggressiveness, negating the privations suffered by others and creating expectations of untrammeled freedom at odds with mature behavior.

The principle of inclusion: *Creating opportunity for those long excluded.* The prosperity of ordinary people is the sun around which a democratic economy orbits. That points to a principle of inclusion for those long excluded—most profoundly, racial inclusion after centuries of racial extraction. A democratic economy sensibility calls on us to recognize the racialized bedrock on which our economic system was built. As we look to the days of the system in its infancy, we can better understand the pitiless gaze of capitalism that did not shrink from reducing persons to "property," commodity goods with no inherent dignity.

The extractive economy carries in its genetic code the ethos of its founders—brutal men like Carnegie, Gould, Vanderbilt, and Rockefeller—who mirrored the ethos of the 19th century. It was an age of enslavement of black people and genocide of Native Americans, a time when women were denied rights of citizenship, and when workers were shot for attempting to organize. It was a social order permeated with biases based on race, sex, and wealth.

The principle of place: *Building community wealth that stays local.* The work of building a democratic economy is grounded in loyalty to geographic place. The real economy of jobs and families and the land always lives someplace local. Cities and towns are places people care passionately about, where working together for the common good instinctively makes sense.

The democratic economy begins with building community wealth of many kinds: social networks, the built environment, cultural riches, individual skills, ecological assets. Keeping this wealth local means using locally rooted ownership, ideally held broadly, to create resilient, shared prosperity. Community wealth creation is fed by the power of institutions anchored in place, like hospitals, universities, and colleges, which represent more than $1.7 trillion in economic activity—close to 9 percent of US GDP. That's more than the agriculture, utilities, and mining sectors put together and roughly equal to the information sector.[22] As nonprofit anchors take up an anchor mission—buying, hiring, and investing locally—money recirculates in the community, creating a multiplier effect, generating greater community stability and well-being.[23]

By contrast, globalization and financialization are the hallmarks of the extractive economy. The place that drives this economy is no place at all, for it embodies a worldview of a generic, commodified economy, where investments cross borders with the click of a mouse, where firms are objects lured from place to place by the $100 billion in government incentives given annually in the US.[24] Enterprise ownership is largely absentee and elite, with the wealthiest 10 percent holding 84 percent of stocks.[25] Benefits are said to trickle down, when actually the system extracts wealth up from communities and sets it spinning in the ethereal realm of speculative trading.

The principle of good work: *Putting labor before capital.* In a democratic economy, good work at a living wage is a central aim. Workers are to be accorded dignity and work itself is honorable—a vital part of developing what philosopher Martha Nussbaum calls full human "capabilities."[26] Economic and political freedoms reinforce one another. Labor comes before capital. This principle was articulated by Abraham Lincoln, who observed that labor is "the superior of capital," deserving "much the higher consideration."[27]

In the extractive economy, income to capital is to be maximized; income to labor is to be minimized. This mandate is embedded in the structure of the income statement, which defines income to capital as *profit,* something to be increased, while income to labor is defined as an *expense,* to be endlessly decreased. A similar bias is found in corporate purpose focused on gains to capital, board membership limited to capital, and a culture of investing that defines maximum income to capital as the prime aim.[28] As the custom has it, no amount of investment income is ever enough. This bias toward capital leads to the ongoing effort to expel labor income from the system, however possible.

The principle of democratized ownership: *Creating enterprise designs for a new era.* In a democratic economy, enterprises are understood to be human communities. Ownership resides with different publics, which could be the workers, the community, the municipal authority, or where appropriate, investors. Various forms of public, private, cooperative, employee, and common ownership are structured at different scales and in different sectors to create the beneficial outcomes we seek. Democratized ownership does not simplistically mean direct voting on managerial decisions. Governance design is appropriate to the living purpose of each enterprise, with proper authority delegated to management, as is required by any efficient operation.

If our economy is to become fit for an era of ecological constraints, enterprise design will evolve away from extractive design. In today's ownership design, corporations are short-term in orientation, require endless growth, measure success by profit and share price, externalize costs onto the environment and, too often, are amoral in decision making. Democratic enterprises are appropriately scaled, with living missions and with decision making by moral agents—which is more likely when ownership is locally rooted and close to daily operations.[29]

Rather than seeing enterprises as living systems, the extractive economy views them as pieces of property to be owned and sold by the propertied class. Workers are economically disenfranchised, much as women and blacks were once politically disenfranchised.[30]

The principle of sustainability: *Protecting the ecosystem as the foundation of life.* In the extractive economy, sustainability conversations with corporations and investors must fit within the frame of profit maximization, showing how to make more money through sustainable practices. The founding generation of America did not trim their arguments to the pleasure of the monarch. They articulated truths held to be self-evident. That's what the UN Brundtland Report did in defining sustainability as meeting present needs without compromising the ability of those in the future to meet their needs.[31]

This is a new economic morality, and in a world of sustainability, everything must fit itself within *this* frame. It is the perspective of the whole—the only perspective consistent with the new physics, which teaches us the world is not a collection of objects but a communion of subjects. Humans are not masters of the earth but members of it.

The extractive economy is waging a war on nature, not so much deliberate as it is heedless, for impact on the natural world is simply invisible. When a stream is damaged by mountaintop removal of coal, for example, the damage is off-screen to financial statements. Since the stream is not an asset owned by the mining company, the enterprise has no fiduciary duty to maintain it. Stream damage is not considered "material." Financial statements tell us: gains to capital owners are real. Tons of debris dumped into a stream that has flowed for thousands of years and may never flow again—that is not real.

The principle of ethical finance: *Investing and lending for people and place.* In ethical finance, social and ecological benefit is the aim. Making money results when this is done well. Responsible banking institutions and impact investing have vital roles to play in bringing money back to the real world, reaching actual companies to fund operations, diminishing the casino economy of speculative trading. In a world of inequality and ecological fragility—with limitless growth not possible—how income is allocated becomes more critical. Ethical investors begin to recognize a moral obligation to limit wealth accumulation. Banks and monetary authorities seek to deploy assets to create resilient ecosystems, build assets for the many, and grow the institutions of the democratic economy. This is the prudent investor, reimagined.

In the extractive economy, capital seeks to enjoy maximum income while bearing little cost for negative consequences. Decision-making power over investments is wielded by financial managers, who maintain that power only by delivering maximum returns. Thus, neither the managers nor the owners of capital feel responsible for the system's ill effects. Those within the system—corporate executives, investment advisors, wealth holders, foundation executives—are often quite caring, yet feel compelled to act as the system demands. When the first moral duty is a fiduciary duty to maximize returns on investments, in effect it becomes the only duty, requiring all other concerns—the well-being of communities, employees, and the environment—to be justified in terms of impact on capital.

STRICT AND NURTURANT

The concept of a democratic economy bridges the divide between progressive and conservative ways of understanding the world—the conservative focus on strictness blended with the liberal focus on nurturance.[32] A democratic economy includes the strictness of financial accountability but also requires ecological accountability, which is ecological strictness. It includes nurturant concern for the common good, yet values the individual freedom to flourish, an aim embraced by both conservatives and liberals.

A democratic economy is a maturation of both worldviews. It is this deep moral structure that makes these principles, this new paradigm, a compass in difficult times.

In outlining these various principles, we're presenting ideals, fully aware that the real world is messy. Most of us step in it more often than we soar on wings. In our work at The Democracy Collaborative, and in every project we write about, everyone is making huge mistakes. How could we not, when everything is being reinvented? This work is not about perfection. A great wave is rising, but it's not carrying us effortlessly where we wish to go. As one participant in the San Francisco circle said, "We ourselves are the tsunami."

2

THE PRINCIPLE OF COMMUNITY

THE COMMON GOOD COMES FIRST

Regenerative community in Indian country

We are the original people.... We have a message for the world.

—JAMES RATTLING LEAF, SICANGU LAKOTA

Nick Tilsen stood at the front of the bus on the side of a road, gesturing out a side window toward the Wounded Knee memorial. "You can't really see through the downpour, but there it is," he said.

It was a darkening afternoon in late May 2015, and we were there on the bus with some Democracy Collaborative colleagues and

20 Native American leaders who were part of our Learning/Action Lab, a multiyear project to aid these leaders in launching or expanding social enterprises and employee-owned companies.[1] *Our visit to Pine Ridge Indian Reservation in South Dakota had been planned months earlier, so Nick was gamely leading this tour—despite the squall now raging in full fury. He stood silently a moment, as we looked out through the lashing rain.*

It was not clear what we expected, but this wasn't it. We could see an arched gateway of wrought iron, and beyond it, a rise leading uphill, seemingly toward nothing—an open expanse. There were no guides greeting people, no kiosks with postcards. No places even to sit. A single weathered obelisk stood against the sky. We couldn't see it through the sheets of rain, but we knew the grounds hold a mass grave surrounded by a chain-link fence, marking the trench where in 1890 the bodies of 300 Lakota men, women, and children were heaped after being gunned down by the US 7th Cavalry.

In history, Wounded Knee looms large. It's the place of the final violent confrontation with the final tribe on the final day—four days after Christmas—of America's long war against its original peoples. It is also where, in 1973, the American Indian Movement (AIM) waged a 71-day standoff with federal marshals, demanding an investigation of broken treaties and government mishandling of Native American assets. This land is drenched with history.

Huddling there in our seats—many of us hadn't packed for the cold on this spring trip—there was an unspoken gratitude that we couldn't get out. Walking these grounds would have felt like being a voyeur, like touching a wound still raw.

Massacres have become disturbingly routine in our day, carried out by solitary madmen with guns or homemade bombs. Here the gunmen numbered 500, and they weren't mad but were sent by a society bent on eradicating a "savage" people, hunting and shooting them down just as they did the buffalo. Native Americans fell beneath America's rush to fulfill the manifest destiny of frontier conquest, so integral to the creation myth of the US—the nation Thomas Jefferson proclaimed contained enough free land "for our descendants to the hundredth and thousandth generation."[2] For millennia, Native Americans had roamed this land, yet the courts would declare it unowned. Lincoln, in his seemingly magnanimous Homestead Act, gave it freely to white settlers.

If the cavalry fired the guns of Wounded Knee, it was the "golden spike" completing the Continental Railroad that proved to be the demise of the Native economy. As Charles Francis Adams, president of the Union Pacific, put it, "The Pacific railroads have settled the Indian question."[3] It was here that one American economy gave way to another, as the railroad kings and their financiers—men like Vanderbilt, Carnegie, Gould, and Morgan—built the iron roads of the rising industrial economy, the seedbed of today's extractive economy. Prospectors came westward to strike it rich, as California and the Black Hills of South Dakota were found to contain, in the words of Sioux holy man Black Elk, the "yellow metal" that white men "worship and that makes them crazy."[4]

The community-based economy of Native Americans—their way of living lightly on the land—nearly vanished here, along with the 30 million buffalo that had once filled these plains, only scattered ghosts of which remained by the time of the Wounded Knee massacre.

BUILDING THE DEMOCRATIC ECONOMY IN INDIAN COUNTRY

Today, the buffalo are beginning to return. There on the bus with us was someone working to make that happen—Mark Tilsen, Nick's father. Creating democratic businesses was his chosen vehicle for change.

Mark and his business partner, Karlene Hunter, had developed the Tanka Bar, a buffalo meat stick cured the traditional Native way with cranberries, which made chemical preservatives unnecessary. They'd started Native American Natural Foods (NANF), a company that had grown to millions of dollars in sales, and whose products had found their way into thousands of stores, including Whole Foods and Costco. The company bought 25 percent of its buffalo from Native producers, with a goal of 100 percent. Believing that asset ownership was critical to economic independence for Native families, Mark and Karlene shared partial equity ownership in their firm with employees, a transition The Democracy Collaborative helped facilitate.

The Tanka Bar pioneered an entirely new category of meat snack. It was so successful it attracted fierce competitors, like the Epic buffalo bar by General Mills, whose packaging claimed it was "shaman blessed." "I even read they named their dog 'Lakota,'" Karlene said.[5]

As NANF battled for shelf space with food conglomerates, it was struggling yet still managing to survive. Mark had turned his hand to a new form of democratic company: a cooperative of Native buffalo producers, Tanka Resilient Agriculture. "Part of our mission is to bring buffalo back to the reservation, to bring buffalo back to the plains," he told our group.

✦ ✦ ✦

Wounded Knee was where Mark had begun his path in "Indian country"—a phrase he and Nick used often. Mark's father had been a prominent civil rights attorney in St. Paul, Minnesota, who defended AIM protesters after Wounded Knee. Mark and his wife Joann Tall met at Wounded Knee.

"My mom was part of the spiritual revival that happened here," Nick said from the front of the bus. "If Wounded Knee hadn't happened, I wouldn't have happened."

As Nick spoke, his words were nearly drowned out by a hailstorm that had abruptly begun pelting the bus like machine-gun fire. "Seventeen Congressional medals of honor were given to the cavalry for what they did here," Nick raised his voice to say. "The marker here used to say, 'The Battle of Wounded Knee,' but a board was put over it, changing it to 'Massacre.' Some people believe this was where our people's spirit was broken." He paused. "It was also where a way was rekindled."

DESIGNING A BETTER SOCIETY

When our Learning/Action Lab first convened in a hotel conference room in Oakland, California, in 2013, Nick showed up as this young guy in a T-shirt and jeans with a quick smile and a dark braid down his back. We soon learned he was part of a youth revival of traditional spiritual practices on Pine Ridge. The regenerative community he was building had been praised publicly by President Barack Obama and would be visited by Julian Castro, the then-US Secretary of Housing and Urban Development. Nick had pulled together an extraordinary, collaborative team to help, including luminaries like Bob Berkebile of BNIM—a leading green architecture and planning firm based in Kansas City, Missouri—who'd done the architectural drafting for the regenerative community. Those drawings would hang in the Cooper Hewitt Smithsonian Design Museum on Manhattan's Upper East Side as part of the exhibit, "By the People: Designing a Better America."[6]

In the five years we worked with Nick, we watched him come into his power, being named an Ashoka Fellow, helping Pine Ridge win designation as a Promise Zone, giving talks around the country, negotiating millions in federal grants, growing his staff from three to more than forty. He was led by—and led others by—a vision rooted in spiritual practice.

There was a time, up until 1978, when certain indigenous religious traditions were outlawed on reservations. The movement to revive these traditions attracted young people like Nick; together they built sweat lodges and learned the Lakota language and ceremonial songs. "Each time we came out of ceremony, we were becoming empowered culturally," Nick told *Indian Country Today*. "We began to recognize a disconnect in what was taught in our ceremonies and what was happening out in our communities. We recognized a welfare mentality. We were holding our hand out, waiting for people to put something in it."[7]

Tribal nations had for countless generations been self-sufficient. After 90 percent of the Native population was wiped out by disease and genocide, with the remaining few pushed onto reservations, their way of life was reshaped around dependency on government support. With families devastated, land lost, and traditions crushed, cultural trauma set in.

It's manifest today in rampant alcoholism, high youth suicide rates, and massive poverty. Pine Ridge is one of the poorest areas in America, with little infrastructure, few jobs, and tribal government as the only major economic engine.

In their spiritual practices, the young people received a message from the elders, Nick said. "How long are you going to let other people decide the future for your children? Are you not warriors? And they said, "It's time to stop talking and start doing. Don't come from a place of fear. Come from a place of hope."

Nick and others decided to found Thunder Valley Community Development Corporation (CDC), a nonprofit organization independent from tribal government.[8] They spent hundreds of hours in listening and planning sessions with community members, creating a vision for the future. "For the first time, they were being asked what they want, not being told what others think they need," Nick said. As the development moved forward, engineers, architects, and foundations supported the effort, including Northwest Area Foundation, Enterprise Community Partners, and the Minnesota Housing Partnership. Funding came from the US Departments of Agriculture and Housing and Urban Development, the South Dakota governor's office, and other sources. Thunder Valley worked with many other organizations on Pine Ridge, including the Lakota Funds, Oglala Sioux Housing Authority, and Wild Horse Butte CDC.[9] At every step, the vision and building of the regenerative community arose from and within many circles of community.

The result was the design for the $60 million regenerative community that Thunder Valley CDC is now building on 34 acres that it owns.[10] This master-planned village is bringing desperately needed affordable homes and rentals, as well as amenities like powwow grounds, an outdoor amphitheater, and youth spaces such as a playground, basketball courts, and a skate park. The plan calls for residents to help build their own homes, their sweat equity helping them save money.

"The entire development is a regenerative, sustainable system," Nick explained. "Every house is positioned to take in the maximum amount of passive solar. There will be 100 percent water reclamation. Building materials are sustainable. It will be a net zero community, producing all the energy it uses."

In a community where unemployment has been estimated to be as high as 85 percent—where every time a dollar hits the reservation, it exits within 48 hours—the regenerative community will feature stores, spaces for incubating Native-owned businesses, and a workforce training center.[11] Youths get construction skills training as homes are built, and Thikáǧa Construction, an employee-owned company, has been launched. Thunder Valley also created a social enterprise program to launch multiple Indian-owned businesses. The first was Thunder Valley Farms, which in late 2017 took delivery of 500 squawking chickens—a step toward food sovereignty for a community whose residents previously had to drive 80 miles to buy chicken that wasn't processed, breaded, and in the freezer section. A group of women on the reservation also formed the Owíŋža Quilters Cooperative.[12]

As Nick puts it, *regeneration* means the ability of an organism to regrow or restore an original function that has been lost. What Thunder Valley is building is not just homes and other structures. It aims to regenerate many kinds of wealth: community spirit, youth skills, food sovereignty, economic self-sufficiency. It's empowering families to take responsibility for their future. "This regenerative community can be seen as a living laboratory" for alleviating poverty and building sustainable communities, Nick said. "It is potentially a national and even international model."[13]

+ + +

Thunder Valley is building community wealth. That's the frame that our project brought to its participants and one that many told us fits naturally with Native American culture. As one participant put it, "what people call a 'new economy' is really a return to what our ancestors always knew."

As the Learning/Action Lab took shape, we at The Democracy Collaborative made our share of mistakes. Initially, we thought our role was to lecture these Native leaders, and at our first gathering, we had multiple PowerPoints at the ready. Participants mutinied, and we were quickly shown the door. With us out of the room, they discussed what they needed. A few hours later they invited us back in, and together we explored how to shift to a practice of *colearning*. We replaced lectures with panels of visiting experts who met one-on-one with participants in personal consultations.

At another point, Marjorie and our colleague Sarah McKinley, who became director of the project, created a bookmark for the group with the web address for our toolkits. We asked our staff designer to add a feather design on one side. When we handed it out, the group immediately began teasing us. "Slap a feather on it" became a standing joke about failed cultural relevance. (We have a stack of unused bookmarks, if anyone's interested.)

Something we did get right was working in a circle, under the skillful facilitation of Jill Bamburg, the president of Pinchot University (today called Presidio Graduate School), now retired, who was part of the project team. Jill made a point of getting each voice into the room at the start and end of each gathering. And we always began with a prayer by a participant, often Nick. (In the 1934 book, *Black Elk Speaks,* Sioux leader Black Elk says that "everything an Indian does is in a circle, and that is because the Power of the World always works in circles.... The wind, in its greatest power, whirls. Birds make their nests in circles, for theirs is the same religion as ours." The seasons form a circle, he said, and "The life of a man is a circle from childhood to childhood, and so it is in everything where power moves.")[14]

All of the groups faced enormous challenges. Of the half-dozen projects that began the journey, by year five, several had failed outright, while others succeeded modestly. Staff turnover was high in every group. Still, the circle held. The culture of the group, which was intimate, playful, and alive, remained intact; it was a true community of practice.

MITAKUYE OYASIN, LAKOTA FOR "ALL MY RELATIONS"

At the center of it was the *principle of community*. It's what gives this framework for economic development a deep cultural relevance for Native

Americans. (No need to slap a feather on it.) Bernie Rasmussen, who was part of the cohort as director of the Spokane Tribal Network, wrote to Ted that he was convinced that community wealth building "is already an indigenous model," and that it "will thrive with the right opportunity."[15] That opportunity would present itself, we found.

Stephanie Gutierrez, who served for a time as director of social enterprise at Thunder Valley, was a latecomer to the group. As she brought herself up to speed on the framework of community wealth building, she and Rae Tall, program coordinator for Thunder Valley's Social Enterprise Initiative at the time, began long discussions about it with each other and with members of the Pine Ridge community. Rae translated the frame of community wealth building into Lakota (see Table 1). Stephanie partnered with Kristen Wagner to launch a consulting group, Hope Nation, to take this approach out to the broader Native community. The embrace of the framework by these women, making it their own, was for us a bolt from the blue.

It was followed by another. Nick announced he was stepping down as head of Thunder Valley to launch the NDN Collective, which would work with groups like the two dozen Native nonprofits and 40-plus tribes that had approached Thunder Valley, seeking to create something similar. Nick explained that he aimed to create a multimillion-dollar investing fund, a consulting arm, a foundation, a network, and an advocacy arm, "so we can build a world where there are hundreds of organizations like Thunder Valley out there." NDN is slang for *Indian*, Nick said; the N also stands for Natives. The "D," Nick said, was about defending, developing, decolonizing.[16]

Then we learned that Sharice Davids—at one-time deputy director of Thunder Valley and someone with whom we'd worked closely—had returned to Kansas City, where she was elected to Congress in 2018. She became one of the first two Native American women to take a seat in the US House of Representatives.[17]

✦ ✦ ✦

Before the final meeting of our Learning/Action Lab, Stephanie prepared a document telling how she and Rae had discussed the traditional colonized approach to economic development on the reservation. They began to explore the imprint the extractive economy had left on their land, their people, their way of being.

Yet the community wealth building approach didn't fully resonate until they began a communal process of translation. One coworker told them, "A long time ago wealth wasn't material things, it was about what you could give." In traditional Lakota culture, a warrior was one who gave gifts to those who had the least. Prior to colonization, Stephanie and Rae explained, "if a family couldn't provide for themselves, other members in the *tiospaye* [broader group of families] would help."[18]

The Lakota word for *wealth* means "to live a happy, well-balanced life, a life of physical and mental health, in balance with creation," they wrote. "For Lakota, community connotes both geographic place and kinship," because this culture "is based on kinship and connection to all that is around us: people, plants, animals, the stars, the land." Before colonization, there was "communal ownership of land and extended, matrilineal, nomadic family structures"; this connection to land is still alive today.[19]

Stephanie talked about a training session she'd attended at the Main Street Project in Northfield, Minnesota, which had developed a regenerative, poultry-centered agricultural system. The whole system is circular, she wrote, with "free-range chickens feeding off the land, providing nutrients back into the soil through their waste, feeding off seeds and droppings from crops that can be harvested," starting the cycle again. It was a mirror of the Lakota way from long ago, when they harvested only what they needed, left little waste, and allowed the wisdom of the natural order to flourish.

THE ETHOS OF THE EXTRACTIVE ECONOMY

This ethos of community and kinship with the land is markedly different from that of Vanderbilt, Carnegie, Morgan, and the other founding fathers of the extractive economy. Theirs was an epoch of global colonization by Western powers—a time when it was still acceptable to think of inferior races destined to be ruled. Today's heroic figure of the self-made billionaire carries an echo of that earlier age. At Wounded Knee, the myth of the frontier comes into focus from a different vantage point, with the suffering and resilience of the colonized in the forefront.

The two worldviews that clashed at Wounded Knee were grounded upon two visions of the individual. One is the root concept of modern economics, *homo economicus*, economic man as a rational self-seeking individual optimizing his own interests. Ecological economist Herman Daly and theologian John Cobb critiqued this notion in *For the Common Good*. It was published in 1989, before today's wide-ranging, nontraditional economic theories, but its critique still rings true of orthodox thinking. "Economists typically identify intelligent pursuit of private gain with rationality, thus implying that other modes of behavior are not rational," Daly and Cobb wrote. "It is through rational behavior, which means self-interested behavior, that all benefit the most."

They proposed a contrasting vision of *homo economicus* as "*person-in-community*." "People are constituted by their relationships," they wrote. "We come into being in and through relationships and have no identity apart from them," for how we think and feel, our aspirations and fears, all are shaped socially.[20]

DEEP STORIES

We carry our cultural narratives largely beneath consciousness. Marjorie recalls the day she was returning from one of our gatherings and ran into a participant, Jo White from Thunder Valley, in the security line at the Denver airport. It was late November, just before a holiday weekend. As the two cleared security and headed off in separate directions, Marjorie waved and called out, "I hope you have a happy Thanksgiving!" Then she paused, and asked, "Do you even celebrate Thanksgiving?" Jo laughed and replied, "Yes, we celebrate keeping you guys alive!"

It was a lighthearted moment, and Jo's manner offered assurance no offense was taken. But the moment spoke to the power of narrative: how we navigate in the world using deep stories of which we remain often unaware.

Among the deepest of these stories is the notion of what it means to be an *economic person*. At Thunder Valley, we see how a system can be built around an economic person for whom community is integral to being fully oneself. As the Lakota worldview tells us, self-interest isn't the only value that arises naturally in the human heart. Concern for others is natural. When self-aggrandizement and wealth accumulation predominate in a society, it is culture that makes it so—not inevitable human nature.

The sense of self as person-in-community is natural to most indigenous cultures. Participants in our project came from many tribes. Winona LaDuke—from the Mississippi band of Anishinaabeg of White Earth Reservation—estimated there are 500 million indigenous peoples worldwide. Their worldview is one in which "human beings exist in intimacy and harmony with the natural world," LaDuke wrote. Indigenous ways "are the only sustainable ways of living," she said. "Community is the only thing in my experience that is sustainable ... It's our way home."[21]

✦ ✦ ✦

When Black Elk, a spiritual leader of the Lakota Sioux at the time of the Wounded Knee massacre, told his life story to John Neihardt in *Black Elk Speaks*, he recounted how his spiritual power had been given to him in a vision during an illness at age nine. Years later, Black Elk shared that vision through dance and ceremony, initiating his evolution as a tribal leader. As he told Neihardt, "a man who has a vision is not able to use the power of it until he performs it on the earth for the people to see."[22]

Nick, too, is enacting a vision for people to see. Many today who embrace narratives of apocalypse and dystopia are also enacting visions for others to see and might be mindful of the powers they're invoking.

Something Nick said at the end of one of our gatherings has stayed with us. Over the years, we'd seen him endure relentless hardship. Yet at the end of one gathering, Nick made this offhand remark. "I think the best days for Indian country," he said, "lie ahead."

TABLE 1. A Lakota Translation of Seven Drivers of Community Wealth Building.

DRIVERS	TRADITIONAL ECONOMIC DEVELOPMENT	COMMUNITY WEALTH BUILDING	LAKOTA COMMUNITY WEALTH BUILDING
Place	Aims to attract firms using incentives, which increases the tax burden on local residents	Develops underutilized local assets of many kinds for benefit of local residents	Embraces loyalty to the Oyate (people) and Unci Maka (planet)
Ownership	Supports absentee and elite ownership, often harming locally owned family firms	Promotes local, broad-based ownership as the foundation of thriving local economy	Belongs to the Oyate; the democratization of ownership
Multipliers	Pays little attention to whether money is leaking out of community	Encourages institutional buy-local strategies to keep money circulating locally	Encompasses formal and informal economic activities, such as bartering and trading locally
Collaboration	Excludes local residents from decision making, which is led primarily by government and private sector	Brings many players to the table: nonprofits, philanthropy, anchors, and cities	Keeps the traditions of our virtues to work with one another as one, reaching out to other indigenous peoples, giving and helping as Lakota people can
Inclusion	Counts jobs created, with little regard for wages or who is hired	Aims to create inclusive, living-wage jobs that help all families enjoy economic security	Makes sure all living things are considered; the triple bottom line: people, planet, and prosperity
Workforce	Relies on generalized training programs without focus on linkages to actual jobs	Links training to employment and focuses on jobs for those with barriers to employment	Considers each person and their ability and makes a place for them

DRIVERS	TRADITIONAL ECONOMIC DEVELOPMENT	COMMUNITY WEALTH BUILDING	LAKOTA COMMUNITY WEALTH BUILDING
System	Accepts status quo of wealth inequality, hoping benefits trickle down	Develops institutions and supportive ecosystems to create a new normal of economic activity	Knows the system is circular; in the Lakota way of life, everything is connected; consciously re-creating sustainable communities

PUBLISHED WITH PERMISSION OF STEPHANIE GUTIERREZ, HOPE NATION.

3

THE PRINCIPLE OF INCLUSION

CREATING OPPORTUNITY FOR THOSE LONG EXCLUDED

Incubating equity in Portland economic development

> Negro history testifies to nothing less than the perpetual achievement of the impossible.
>
> —JAMES BALDWIN

Collapse and regeneration are experiences Tyrone Poole knows intimately. There was that period back in 2006 when he was homeless—that moment when, on crutches and in excruciating pain, Tyrone found himself staggering into the bus station in Portland, Oregon, where he collapsed on a bench and threw up. That was how a policeman found him that night and later took him to the YMCA homeless shelter, where he got a cot on the gym floor. Everything he owned was in a bag under the bed.[1]

What had led to Tyrone's downslide was medical debt. He'd completed his associate degree at Portland Community College and was training to be a firefighter when he suffered a debilitating injury. The treatments left him buried under medical bills, evicted, his car repossessed.

As Tyrone told his story, he sat across the conference table in the elegant Williams & Dame Development building on Everett Street, in Portland's hip Pearl District, where his new business has free office space. It's part of the intricate web of support that has come to surround him, the physical embodiment of the community that oriented itself toward growing the seeds of resilience and genius in him. Tyrone is 34, African-American, with a trim beard and close-cropped hair, and on this day he was wearing a green T-shirt and crisp new blue jeans. He's the founder of OneApp, a startup that has launched an online platform originally designed to match applicants for affordable housing with appropriate openings. Tyrone talked about being named Oregon Entrepreneur of the Year, how his team won a contract with the Portland Housing Bureau, and how other cities and states are lining up to tap his services.

None of that seemed in reach when he first hatched his idea. While in the homeless shelter, Tyrone began helping other residents find housing with their vouchers from the city government. Before long, the YMCA hired him as a family advocate.[2] From his own struggles, he'd seen the reality of the statistic that people with housing vouchers have applications turned down by landlords 40 percent of the time.[3] The system left thousands of low-income families stranded—in a system rife with racial discrimination, black residents were three times more likely to be homeless than white Portlanders. A 2011 audit by the Portland Housing Bureau found discrimination against prospective black and Latino tenants by landlords and leasing agents in 64 percent of cases.[4]

Tyrone saw it as a math problem. He developed an algorithm that could match applicants with openings. "There's little you know about how you fared on the screening criteria," Tyrone explained, because those criteria are undisclosed. "It may be that if you pay off Sprint and an overdue library book, you'll be OK." With each application costing $30 to $50, a housing search can add up to a painful sum for threadbare pocketbooks.[5]

Tyrone began to develop his idea for the web platform. "I knew it would work," he said, "but I didn't have the business knowledge." Then he learned about the Startup PDX Challenge, a contest for entrepreneurs the Portland Development Commission (PDC), the city's economic development agency, ran for three years.

* * *

Kimberly Branam, executive director of the PDC, explained to us how that contest evolved to support underrepresented entrepreneurs like Tyrone. The original concept was that would-be entrepreneurs could compete to receive a package worth $50,000 that included mentoring, free office space, legal assistance, business planning support, and $10,000 (later increased to $15,000) in a working capital grant.

When the contest's first group of winning founders was gathered together, Kimberly recalled, "We looked around the room, and they were largely white men."[6] The next year, the PDC refocused the contest on underrepresented founders, primarily women and people of color. It was one move in what would become a wholesale reorientation of the PDC toward racial and gender inclusion—not as one piece of its mission, but as its new core.

The city realized how important it was to provide seed capital and mentoring at very early stages for underrepresented founders, so in 2015, it put out a request for proposals, looking for fund managers willing to manage an early-stage seed fund for these founders. The $2 million fund was launched in partnership with PDC, Multnomah County, and the State of Oregon and was the first publicly backed preseed fund in the country, to which the city contributed $750,000.[7]

When Kimberly became director in 2017, she led the agency's rebranding as Prosper Portland to reflect its reorientation to focusing on the traditionally disadvantaged. "Building an Equitable Economy" was the new goal. The challenge, the agency explained on its website home page, was "[t]he growing income and asset disparity between white people and people of color. Solution: Collaborate to grow jobs and increase assets among communities of color."[8]

We first encountered Kimberly a few years earlier, when she spoke at one of our Learning/Action Labs for Native Americans. What was striking to us was her frank acknowledgment of how the agency's own work had contributed to racial exclusion. We learned that she'd talked about this not only to our small group, but at the massive Social Capital Markets conference held annually in the Bay Area. In a presentation titled "A Tale of Two Cities," she'd spoken about how the progressive image of Portland was belied by a stark racial divide to which city economic development had actively contributed. Something remarkable seemed to be happening in Portland—a powerful, citywide pilot in the *principle of inclusion*. It warranted a journey there to learn more.

BUILDING HIS TEAM, OVERCOMING HURDLES

Far from considering himself a self-made man, Tyrone credits the large team of helpers he's assembled. For example, when he hit his first stumbling block in the $150 application fee for the PDX Challenge, Tyrone found help from Stephen Green, business development officer with the City, himself a prominent black entrepreneur. He was "my saving grace," Tyrone said.[9]

Then came social obstacles. "I remember going to the first mixer PDC hosted for the Challenge," Tyrone recalled. "There were people there with logos and matching T-shirts" speaking a jargon-filled language he found intimidating. "Everyone was mingling. I mingled with no one," he said.

At each step of the process, Tyrone expected to be eliminated. "I remember my first pitch ever," he recalled. "Everyone had handouts with diagrams, graphs, and PowerPoints." He had a tablet with a single piece of paper. "I ran to the copy machine to copy things. I had on my only suit, and I was sweating so bad, my suit was soaked." His pitch that day proved so compelling, it advanced him to the top 20 out of 150.

"I work at a place where 50 percent of the families will be out on the street, even though they have a letter from the city government authorizing access to housing," Tyrone explained. "When I got out of the hospital myself, I qualified for 1 percent of all available housing—10 out of 1,000. That's like finding a needle in a haystack. Do you know how much time it takes to find a needle in a haystack? If it exceeds the amount of money and time a family has, it will result in denial of housing. Every application, every screening, costs resources that the people who are applying have in short supply. The two moving pieces have to match up. I can reduce the information to one platform. With one click, an applicant can be screened against all available homes."

Tyrone became one of the six winners, receiving a $15,000 cash grant and other services. His challenges had only begun.

"I didn't need cash," he explained. "What I needed was a clue, how to make this idea a reality." The development commission connected him with a mentor, Jon Maroney of the Oregon Angel Fund (OAF)—a group created in 2007 to invest $100 million in 100 local startups, with an aim of creating 10,000 jobs in Oregon. "He gave me a check for $25,000," Tyrone said, which was used to create a beta site. "It was trash," he added with a laugh, but it demonstrated proof of concept.

"The most important thing Prosper Portland gave me was validity," he continued. "That social capital, I was able to use it like it was capital." There was the time TransUnion, a large credit rating firm, denied him access to the credit scores he needed for his platform. Then development staffer Katherine Krajnak asked Kimberly to draft a letter. "The next thing you know, TransUnion gave me the credit database," he said. "This is information that you can go to prison for misusing; they gave it to me, a nobody, because of the City of Portland."

✦ ✦ ✦

"You have to go to bat for folks," Katherine emphasized, when we sat down with her later. "This is about more than setting up programs." Katherine is one of the project managers for the entrepreneurship program at Prosper Portland, and as she joined us at the agency's small meeting room, she'd just come from a meeting of the Equity Council, an internal working group on inclusion. She talked about how trainings brought staff through exercises to get in touch with unconscious biases. "You have to examine yourself as a white person, or as a man, or as an able-bodied person," Katherine explained. People are asked to *caucus*—gather with others of the same color or gender—to "see how we each internalize superiority or inferiority. Why does one person feel entitled to interrupt another, or talk over them?" Why do some not speak? "There's internalized oppression," she said.[10]

Underrepresented groups can include women, people of color, veterans, and the disabled. "Women business owners' have average revenue that's one-fifth that of men," Katherine said. "There are plenty of women-owned businesses, but they're not growing." She talked about how a body isn't healthy if half isn't working. "If my right arm and right leg don't work, I'm not a fully functioning human," she said.[11] When some neighborhoods or certain kinds of potential business leaders lack opportunity, the entire city is affected. Conversely, studies show that when there is less segregation by race and income, regions enjoy longer periods of economic prosperity.[12]

✦ ✦ ✦

The principle of inclusion is fundamental to creating a democratic economy designed for the flourishing of each and all. In such an economy, Tyrone's perspective as a once-homeless person becomes an asset to be developed. He, in turn, takes a market approach, not a social service approach, to helping the low-income. Inclusion is thus built into basic economic processes: entrepreneurship, economic development, product development. That's fundamental to democratic economy design; social purpose isn't added on but is at the core.

This is a very different approach from giving welfare to the disadvantaged while giving economic development assistance to wealthy whites, as in today's economy. Such an approach reflects an implicit belief that stigmatized groups cannot advance "the progress of history," in the words of Martin Luther King, Jr.[13] What is lost is a loss to the whole.

Imagine if Portland had not run this contest, if there had been no mentoring—what would Tyrone's future have been? In our extractive economy, how much talent is left to wither painfully on the vine?

PORTLAND'S TALE OF TWO CITIES

Racism, King reminded us, is not "just an occasional departure from the norm on the part of a few bigoted extremists."[14] If it found its most vicious face in the South, it was manifest elsewhere in the actions of real estate brokers, bankers, employers, policymakers—and, as Kimberly acknowledged, economic development leaders. In 2014, a damning report by Portland State University and the Coalition for Communities of Color found that income for blacks in Portland was half that of whites, and that city and state governments had been slow to dismantle "overtly racist policies."[15]

Those policies flowed from the region's racist past. When Oregon entered the union in 1859, it forbade black people from living there. A subsequent law prevented black people from owning land.[16] Portland's history of urban renewal was cut from the same cloth. In 1956, voters approved the construction of an arena in a largely black neighborhood, Albina, resulting in the destruction of more than 400 homes. Then the PDC (the precursor to Prosper Portland) approved the clearing of vast tracts in northeast Portland to construct highways and Legacy Emanuel Hospital, leaving more than 300 African-American homes and small businesses dislocated.[17]

In setting out to remedy this past, Prosper Portland has at times stumbled. For example, controversy surrounded the Hill Block, part of the area razed for the Legacy hospital, which long stood vacant. When the development agency announced it had secured commitment from Legacy to grant the property to the African-American community and invest in the community process to determine what would occur at the site, residents protested. They feared a deal had been made behind closed doors that wouldn't ultimately help minority businesses. "You've changed your name," local resident Rahsaan Muhammad told the Prosper Portland board, "but you haven't changed your behavior."[18] In working through that controversy, Prosper Portland, Legacy, and the city relied upon a community-led working group and visioning process for the development that they designed together.[19]

That's an example of the active listening Prosper Portland seeks to practice, which can be contentious but potentially healing. Dialogue, rebuilding lost trust, examining one's own biases, admitting past failures: all this is part of the difficult process of inclusion. Essential to this process, in the largest sense, is coming to terms with the racial bedrock on which our economy has been built.

WHAT IS LOST IN THE LANGUAGE OF CAPITAL

The traditional story of capitalism's early days extols Adam Smith's pin factory and the benevolent invisible hand. Black writers tell a different genesis story, focusing on the South's cotton plantations and the brutal hand of racial extraction.

"The land that enslaved people planted in cotton," Harvard professor Walter Johnson wrote, "had been expropriated from the Creek, the Cherokee, the Choctaw, the Chickasaw, and the Seminole." In the emerging capitalist system of the 1800s—which knit together the cotton plantations of Mississippi with the looms of Manchester, England, and the financiers of New York—"[e]nslaved people were the collateral upon which the entire system depended," Johnson noted. As cotton merchants loaned money to planters to finance operations until harvest, they required security. "That security was the value of the enslaved," Johnson said. "*Enslaved people were the capital.* Their value in 1860 was equal to all of the capital invested in American railroads, manufacturing, and agricultural land combined."[20] [Emphasis in original.]

Acknowledging this past helps us see what is lost in the language of capital—how seemingly benign processes like securitization and protection of property rights can have a dehumanizing underside. Despite widespread revulsion against slavery in the era of abolition, it was respect for property rights that blocked progress. Even after emancipation, it was the planters who were paid for their loss of property. "No one compensated the slaves," historian Catlin Rosenthal wrote; "the enslaved were never seen as the ones who had been expropriated."[21]

A democratic economy recognizes the rights of property, yet balances those with other human rights—an inclusive right to human flourishing, the primary aim of protecting the common good, the moral obligation to atone for harms committed. Building an inclusive economy is part of the long movement away from bias of every kind toward creating a society that serves the well-being of all.

TAKING INCLUSION TO SCALE IN ECONOMIC DEVELOPMENT

Embracing inclusion is about cultivating empathy, as the leaders of Prosper Portland are seeking to do. Since running the contest that Tyrone won, Prosper Portland has evolved a broader ecosystem to support underrepresented entrepreneurs—the Inclusive Business Resource Network, which partners with others to offer programs such as microloans, seed funding, business loans, legal support, accounting, and market research. These services are offered to business owners of color, immigrants, women founders, and other underrepresented entrepreneurs, reaching 600 businesses each year. Prosper Portland's plan for 2017 and 2018 was to invest $2.5 million among the network providers, with an aim of seeing 1,000 businesses strong and stabilized by 2022.[22]

Portland isn't alone in this kind of work. Seattle, Milwaukee, and Madison, Wisconsin, are also taking steps to advance racial economic equity. Cites like these come together in the Government Alliance on Race and Equity, a national network in which 50 city, state, and regional governments are pursuing racial equity work.[23]

If racial inclusion is vital, by itself it's not sufficient—a point Martin Luther King, Jr. emphasized in his final years. As he planned his Poor People's Campaign, his focus was widening to embrace economic justice for all who are dispossessed. He became increasingly outspoken in his dissatisfaction with capitalism and was in Memphis to support 1,300 striking garbage collectors when he was shot.[24]

In the period leading up to this, King shared a growing sense of unease with Harry Belafonte. "We have fought long and hard for integration," he told Belafonte. And King said he felt confident about winning. But without economic justice for all—without transformation of the system itself—King said he feared "I am integrating my people into a burning house."[25]

✦ ✦ ✦

After our visit to Portland, we saw in the *Portland Business Journal* that Tyrone's platform was live and 5,000 Portland families had accessed it. He'd succeeded in landing $2.25 million from investors by the close of 2018—bringing the company's total investment to about $3.5 million. The funds were from individual angel investors, with about 50 angels in total backing the enterprise, many of them people of color. Tyrone had pitched many institutional investors and venture funds, but they hadn't written checks. "The opportunity for minorities in these funds doesn't exist," Tyrone told the *Journal*. According to research firm CB Insights, only about 1 percent of the billions invested by venture capital funds goes to African-American founders.[26]

The article brought to mind something Tyrone had said when he'd first walked into the conference room where we waited. "I'm sorry I won't be able to talk for as long as we originally scheduled," he said. "One of my angel investors is on life support and a group of her family and friends are meeting around her bedside to say goodbye." He'd promised us an hour, and we ended up having 45 minutes. Something important was calling.

4

THE PRINCIPLE OF PLACE

BUILDING COMMUNITY WEALTH THAT STAYS LOCAL

The $13 billion anchor mission in Cleveland

> [T]he crucial and perhaps only and all-encompassing task is to understand place, the immediate specific place where we live.
>
> —KIRKPATRICK SALE

"I was going strong and then I got the meeting," Daniel said. After working three years at the plant of a multinational corporation in Cleveland, he was laid off. "It was a full-production plant, but they were doing a lot of cutbacks. We were told they had $3 million to cut." Soon after, Daniel saw a flyer for Step Up to UH, a recruitment and training program run by University Hospitals as a path to employment for residents from nearby low-income

neighborhoods. Daniel was in his 30s, African-American, wearing a blue uniform. As he talked, he sat across the table in the Employee Enrichment Center in the hospital's Lerner Tower. He told about how he was accepted into the Step Up program, how it taught him soft skills, like how to dress, how to accept supervision without defensiveness. He sought out work at the nonprofit hospital, he explained, because "It's more stable." As someone with four children, he "had to think stability. The hospital isn't going anywhere."[1]

After graduating from Step Up in 2015, Daniel started at University Hospitals (UH) as an environmental services worker at $11 an hour. (Step Up asked that Daniel's last name not be used.) Within a year and a half, he advanced to $13.13 an hour. He's now studying accounting, and UH is paying for his classes. "I'm going for a CPA, I've always been good with numbers," Daniel said, settling back in his chair, his eyes taking on a deeper intensity. "I'm in here all the time," he added, gesturing toward the half-dozen computers for employee use. "I'm looking at the job board, waiting for the next time an entry-level accounting position opens up."

Daniel's path—from a laid-off factory worker to an accounting degree—is the kind of trajectory of hope University Hospitals is interested in. This nonprofit hospital system goes out of its way for Daniel, one among 26,000 employees, because of *the principle of place*. This institution cares about the neighborhoods surrounding its flagship medical center on Euclid Avenue—where unemployment is a dismal 24 percent, closer to 40 percent counting discouraged workers. These are among the most disinvested areas in a city where poverty overall stands at 39 percent.[2]

University Hospitals is rooted here. This nonprofit hospital system has revenues of a massive $3.9 billion.[3] While traditional corporations of such size operate anywhere and everywhere, their gaze fixed on Wall Street, University Hospitals is focused on northeast Ohio, where it's operated since 1866.

The heart of UH is found at Cleveland's University Circle—a square mile oasis of dozens of world-class educational, cultural, and health institutions, including Cleveland Clinic, Case Western Reserve University, and UH. These three institutions alone represent more than $13 billion in annual economic activity.[4] Little of it traditionally reached their immediate community. Head out from their pristine world in your car, and within minutes you'll come across long-empty buildings that are graffiti-covered, with glass blown out, windows staring vacantly across weed-choked lots.

Those neighborhoods are where the Evergreen Cooperative Laundry was launched. The laundry is twelve minutes by car from University Hospitals. Many Evergreen employees were hired from these neighborhoods. The large contracts fueling the three Evergreen businesses were made by anchor institutions like Case Western Reserve University, UH, and Cleveland Clinic. How this came to be is a story of how social breakdown and separation can become soil for seeds of renewal and connection. It's a story with profound lessons for the emergence of the democratic economy.

In particular, it's a story about how government alone isn't enough to pull the disadvantaged into economic well-being. Anchor institutions are another source of substantial economic power that potentially puts the interests of people and community first.

FROM SEGREGATION TO CONNECTION

At one time the institutions of University Circle were radically disconnected from their neighbors. In a city that today remains the most segregated in America,[5] these neighborhoods were the less desirable areas to which blacks were effectively limited in the early twentieth century's Great Migration from the South to escape the harshness of Jim Crow. Later, as manufacturing jobs left the Rust Belt for low-wage areas, unemployment in Cleveland grew. These neighborhoods deteriorated.

University Circle institutions experienced vandalism, a few attacks on women, visitors reluctant to come to the area. Many professionals moved to the suburbs. In the citadel of the area's large institutions, the talk was of an urban decay they feared might engulf them. When urban renewal was attempted, it was often about razing dwellings for institutional expansion. The areas around University Circle became a tinderbox of racial resentment. Then, in 1966 and 1968, what were then called race riots erupted within a mile of the district. Today Cleveland residents call them rebellions.[6]

White residents and businesses increased their flight. The institutions withdrew—focusing on their missions of healing the sick and educating the elite, not on helping their neighbors. Today this history remains visible in the area's brutalist architecture, where concrete, bunker-style buildings offer first-floor walls that are blank and inaccessible—silently voicing the divide of us versus them.[7]

This legacy confronted Ronn Richard when he became president of the Cleveland Foundation in 2003. His wife, Bess Rodriguez Richard, began volunteering at the Cleveland School of the Arts, across from the Cleveland Museum of Art, where admission is free. One day, Bess mentioned a museum exhibit connected to the day's lesson and asked students if they'd seen it. Not a hand went up. One student finally said, "Miss Bess, that's not for us."[8]

Shaken, Bess told this story to her husband. The next day, Ronn reached out to the heads of local anchor institutions. It was the beginning of the Greater University Circle Initiative (GUCI), which, more than a decade later, remains an ongoing network of anchors using their economic power to benefit the place they call home.

Ronn shared his vision of a "new geography of collaboration"—*Greater* University Circle, in which anchors and neighbors form a single community. It captured a growing consensus that the futures of the institutions and neighborhoods were inextricably linked. A vibrant neighborhood adds to an institution's viability. When the community suffers, institutions cannot thrive. GUCI proved the truth of something Martin Luther King, Jr. had said, that we're woven together in "an inescapable network of mutuality, tied into a single garment of destiny."[9]

At first GUCI's focus was physical development. Anchors found together they could raise funds at great scale—for projects like Uptown, a $150 million mixed-use development that revitalized a moribund stretch of Euclid Avenue.[10] GUCI's goals expanded to become Buy Local, Hire Local, Live Local, and Connect. Today among its legacies it counts increased enrollment at Case Western Reserve University, hundreds of employees who've moved back to the area, and 28 brownfields remediated. There's the NewBridge training facility, where more than 600 people have been trained, and the Health Tech Corridor, with 1,800 local jobs retained and 1,300 jobs created. There's the Neighborhood Connections program and its Network Nights, connecting neighborhood residents to each other and to the institutions.[11] GUCI is today strategizing new directions and has asked The Democracy Collaborative to help.

MAKING IT UP AS YOU GO ALONG

Perhaps GUCI's most innovative program was the Evergreen Cooperative initiative. Its three worker-owned businesses launched between 2009 and 2012, of which the laundry is one, were initially designed to meet the purchasing needs of local anchors.

It began the day Ted spoke at a roundtable on community wealth building he helped organize in Cleveland. If India Pierce Lee from the Cleveland Foundation hadn't heard him that day, our lives would be very different now. Afterward, she invited The Democracy Collaborative to do a feasibility study on an anchor strategy to help low-income neighborhoods. Our former colleague Steve Dubb and Ted did more than 100 interviews with anchors: What were they buying? What could anchors buy locally? They used the results to design a strategy for employee-owned companies to meet the needs of area colleges and health systems.

As the project began, Ted commuted monthly to Cleveland. "You know, one day you'll be moving here and become one of us," India said at one point. Ted laughed. A year later, he was living in Cleveland.

So, as someone who'd been living (happily) in Metro Washington, DC, he made a new home in this Rust Belt city. He and India and Lillian Kuri of the Cleveland Foundation, along with anchor leaders and a business development team, made it up as they went along. No other city had tried a community wealth building strategy like this. As he became integrated into the community, Ted realized that, everywhere else he'd lived, he'd been disconnected from place and didn't know it.

The approach was naïve at first. When the CEOs of GUCI said "we're all in," we thought that meant the Evergreen Cooperative Laundry had contracts. Then it became clear that in a bureaucracy of 26,000, Joe in procurement didn't care what the CEO said. The hospitals were locked into huge, multiyear contracts. But there were tricks. For example, Steve Standley, chief administrative officer at UH, convinced a large supplier to carve out a subcontract for the Evergreen Cooperative Laundry.

Tracey Nichols, then the director of Cleveland economic development, called up one day. She helped line up financing, which included a $1.5 million Housing and Urban Development (HUD) loan for Evergreen Cooperative Laundry; an $8 million HUD loan and a $2 million HUD grant for Green City Growers; and a $1.5 million state loan for Evergreen Energy Solutions.[12]

It took three years working with anchors before we found a way to really connect with the community. Now there's a richer strategy for engagement. In fact, the motivation for the Step Up to UH program came out of neighborhood dialogue, where people expressed frustration about not being able to get in the door. In retrospect, we should have started at the top and bottom at the same time.

ORGANIZING 800-POUND PLAYERS

Anchor support was vital for the Evergreen Cooperatives, but also not enough. Evergreen Energy Solutions got its start installing large solar arrays at institutions like Case Western Reserve University, but later it had to broaden its business model, taking on painting, home renovations, and LED lighting installation for many clients. Green City Growers sold to nonprofit anchors, but it also needed other local institutional buyers—including an $800,000-a-year contract selling basil to Nestle.[13] The greenhouse for years lost money. Today it's in the black, as are all three worker-owned businesses.

The most substantial anchor impact recently has been at the Evergreen Cooperative Laundry, which in 2018 won a competitive bid to handle all the laundry for Cleveland Clinic. Starting pay at that facility was raised 20 percent over what the previous manager, a multinational firm, had paid. Overnight, 100 new employees were on a fast track to ownership. Employment at Evergreen Cooperative Laundry tripled.[14]

Over time, it's become clear that anchor work is really a sophisticated community organizing strategy. What you're organizing are big institutional players. At The Democracy Collaborative, we're taking this lesson to scale. Our Healthcare Anchor Network has close to 40 major nonprofit hospital systems, collectively employing over 1 million people, with $50 billion in spending on goods and services, and $150 billion in investment assets.[15] They're learning together to be effective anchors for their communities. That network's success inspired us to launch a network of colleges and universities, and a third network of place-based anchor collaboratives.[16]

We're more powerful together than apart. The deep redesign of processes is hard for a bureaucracy, and people need support to risk change in routines. But concern for the people in the place that's home—that's what brings people together. It's the glue.

RETURNING TO THE LOCAL

Returning to place is a way to begin righting the relationship between economy and society. It was the Industrial Revolution that turned that relationship inside out, making industry the ruling force. Throughout prior history, historian Karl Polanyi observed, economic activity had been just one part of a social order encompassing religion, government, families, and the natural world. The kings of capital turned labor and land into market commodities—to be "bought and sold, used and destroyed, as if they were simply merchandise," Polanyi wrote. But they were fictitious commodities, for they were human beings and the earth.[17]

Anchor institutions are part of a return to localism, and part of a reimagining of what it means to create health. These hospitals recognize that healthcare represents only 10 to 20 percent of health outcomes.

More important are the *social determinants of health*—the conditions in which people are born, work, and live. Economic development is a path toward health—as it also prevents unnecessary demand on the health-care system.[18]

The potential for scale is off the charts. Hospitals and universities represent 8.7 percent of US GDP, which is an enormous swath of economic activity.[19] It's equally true that turning these large institutions is as slow as turning a battleship.

GOING AGAINST TRADITION, CONFRONTING SKEPTICISM

After Daniel left the Employee Enrichment Center at UH, we visited Kim Shelnik, vice president of human resources at UH; with her was Staci Wampler, program manager from Towards Employment, which partners on the Step Up program. "This is a very different group to go in and secure employment," Kim explained. "You're employing individuals who never would have had a chance to make it through the normal selection process." She oversees the hiring processes of UH, where 17,000 apply each month for 1,500 to 1,600 openings. "You already have candidates," Kim explained. "You have to put aside openings for this."[20]

We sat in on one Step Up class, where participants were eight women in their late teens and early 20s, all people of color. They were dressed in skirts and stepped out, one by one, for mock interviews. Discussion was about the handout, "Opposing Rules of Home and Work." In personal life, one column read, "I should be able to live by my own set of rules." The instructor asked, "Is this true for you?" Most hands went up. "At work it's different," she explained, reading from the facing column: "Do what you are asked to do, even when you don't want to."[21]

On day nine of this ten-day class, the recruiter will visit. "I expect 100 percent will be made an offer" for a job at UH, instructor Yvette Herod said during break. "Some will decline." Though she tried to explain to them, some don't realize that if they wait, they'll be competing against thousands.

In a normal pool of applicants, Kim said, only 1 out of 69 will be hired. "We had to create a funnel before the funnel to prepare residents." If this seems to go against "the tradition of fair process," she continued, "it's a different kind of fair process." The graduates have been more successful than those from the traditional selection process, with lower turnover. Step Up has made 246 hires in four years, with one-year retention of 73 percent, compared to 66 percent in other hiring. "That's unheard of," Kim said. "That's why we keep it going." The secret is the job coach provided for the first six months, which Kim called "the secret sauce." Coaches help with soft skills, the number one reason for turnover.[22]

Initially, Step Up met skepticism from her colleagues, Kim continued. "But we didn't give up. It was my reputation on the line." Over time, Step Up proved itself to be good business.[23] Yet at the time of our visit, the program was at risk. "To be honest, we can't afford Step Up," Kim said. "It will end unless we find funding." For a few years, the cost was picked up by the Cleveland Foundation. Then a Kellogg grant was found. The annual cost is $25,000 to $28,000, about $1,250 per person.

As Kim related this, Staci turned and reported she had a dozen women starting new classes. Kim paused. Across the face of this woman—struggling with a shortage of registered nurses, facing staff cuts every year in her hiring team—there flit a look of satisfaction, something bordering on happiness. She relaxed. "That's great," she said.

✦ ✦ ✦

As promising as Kim and Staci's work is—and as enormous as University Hospital's and GUCI's resources could potentially be in benefiting community—the truth is, all these efforts struggle upstream against the massive currents of the extractive economy. Looking back to when Daniel was laid off by his previous employer—2014, when his plant needed to cut $3 million—financial statements showed sales worldwide at that multinational were more than $90 billion. That was down slightly from the year prior. Yet profit was up dramatically, from 11 percent to 16 percent.[24]

When revenue falls but profit rises, that means expenses were slashed. The biggest expense is generally labor. Put simply: income to capital is increased by reducing income to labor. This was likely done through cuts across the company's more than 400 factories in over 100 countries. It's not deliberate cruelty. This company is a valuable employer for Cleveland. But like any company with ownership trading in the stock markets, it's constrained by the system design.

Disruption in human lives disappears in the tally of what matters: earnings per share. Profit allocated to shareholders. As journalist Alex Berenson observed, "More than any other number, earnings per share determines whether a company's shares will rise or fall, whether its chief executive will be rewarded or fired, whether it will build a new headquarters or endure a round of layoffs." In short, "Earnings per share is the number for which all the other numbers are sacrificed."[25]

In the year 2014, this corporation's earnings per share rose from $3 to $4, and its stock price soared from $66 to over $70. The year Daniel lost his job, the chairman of the company made $6 million, as pay for performance for a job well done.

5

THE PRINCIPLE OF GOOD WORK

PUTTING LABOR BEFORE CAPITAL

The worker-centered economy of Cooperative Home Care Associates

---

> Work, properly conducted in conditions of human dignity and freedom, blesses those who do it and equally their products.
>
> —E. F. SCHUMACHER

"I never knew how many case hours they would give me each week, and I never had enough hours to make a decent paycheck. They gave me no health insurance, and no benefits." That's how Octaviea Martin, the mother of two young children, described

conditions at the Bronx-based agency where she worked for four years as a home health aide, caring for the disabled and elderly. Her experience is typical of the 1.8 million people who work as home health aides. These workers are 90 percent women, predominantly women of color, most often from immigrant communities. They're commonly on welfare or just off it, often haven't completed high school, and hold jobs of low status in the healthcare system. They face what many millions of workers face today: unstable part-time hours, few or no benefits, little respect.[1]

Then Octaviea found work with Cooperative Home Care Associates (CHCA) in the South Bronx, which is a worker-centered, for-profit company. The difference was stark. At CHCA, she enjoyed steady income, health insurance, personal days off, and people to turn to when she needed help.[2]

CHCA was launched in 1985 as a social experiment in creating good work for home health aides—and, in the process, creating higher-quality care for low-income, frail clients. It's succeeded to a remarkable extent, both as a business and as a model of a democratic economy. It has revenue of more than $65 million and has been in operation for 33 years, with all but three of those being profitable. The company is a cooperative fully owned by its workers and employs a massive 2,300, about half of whom are now owners. And the company is a certified B Corporation, which means it has a mission of serving the common good embedded in its governing framework.

In a community plagued by generations of unemployment, the company recruits and trains more than 600 workers every year and supplies them with a job at the end. Once employed, workers get case managers and peer mentors to help find childcare or navigate immigration concerns and work demands. Workers exercise voice through a union, a labor-management committee, and voting power over 8 out of 14 board seats—seats held by workers themselves. Benefits are generous, and the company is committed to creating full-time work of at least 35 hours a week.

The work is hard and not high paying. Yet workers stay. CHCA's turnover rate, at 20 to 25 percent, is less than half the industry average of 66 percent.[3] The certifying group B Lab has singled out CHCA as one of a small handful of companies deemed "Best for the World," for creating positive social impact.[4]

THE CRISIS OF GOOD WORK

"An island of human decency," CHCA has been called.[5] It is indeed an island in a global extractive economy increasingly hostile to worker prosperity. Pay to workers, even with recent small upticks, has long been stagnant in Europe, the US, Japan, and other wealthy nations.[6] In the US, secure work has given way to insecure, part-time, contract, gig-economy–type labor, with more jobs threatened by advancing automation. The result is a dissolving middle class and the swelling of the working poor. Those lucky enough to retain full-time jobs often face crushing workloads and meaningless work—with bleak prospects ahead for the next generation. We're in the midst of a massive crisis of good work, a degradation of work and workers that's been advancing silently for decades.

Economists scratch their heads over why wages have barely budged in decades, even as unemployment has plummeted; there's little agreement among them on the reasons. The *New York Times* has called it a "mystery" and an "economic puzzle." Researchers point to the decline of unions, globalization, outsourcing, the Uber economy, automation—all seemingly disparate forces. At the 2018 gathering of the European Central Bank in Sintra, Portugal, a telling comment was made by Aviv Nevo, a professor of economics at the University of Pennsylvania. Summing up economists' uncertainty about wage dynamics, he said, "We're all drunks looking under the lamppost."[7]

That's the old joke about looking for missing keys where the light is better rather than where the keys were lost. If we step outside the brightly lit areas of mainstream dialogue, we find the darker fact of increasing extraction by capital and how that's driven by the bias lying hidden behind stagnant wages, bias in favor of capital, and bias against labor, which is part of the logic and rules of the game.

BALANCING MISSION AND MANAGEMENT

CHCA is driven by a different logic—the *principle of good work*. The company mission is emblazoned on a chartreuse wall in its entryway: "Committed to delivering quality care by creating quality jobs." Stepping into CHCA's spotless offices in the gritty South Bronx, one sees on the faces of the receptionists a subtle something. The absence of fear, perhaps. Or the presence of belonging.

"In the 1980s, this was a pretty rough business," said Michael Elsas, seated in an office around the corner from reception. "No one cared about the workers." This white man—with a halo of gray hair and a trim beard, dressed in blue jeans, blazer, and cowboy boots—came to CHCA as president in 2000, serving for 16 years as the firm quadrupled from 500 to today's 2,300 employees. He served as a consultant to CHCA in 2017; today he's retired.[8]

CHCA is now run by a woman of color, Adria Powell, the daughter of cofounder Peggy Powell. Adria began working at the company part-time while in high school. Now in her 40s, she's been president since January 2017. Adria makes $200,000 a year, the same as Michael before her. "The president of the cooperative has never made more than ten times the lowest wage earner, and that continues to be the case for me," she said.[9]

"A multiple of ten is where we should be as a society," Michael said. He pointed, by contrast, to the largest 350 US businesses, where CEO pay today is 271 times that of the average worker.[10]

As strongly mission-oriented as CHCA is, it is first a business. "If you don't manage the company well," Michael said, "you'll have all the bells and whistles of a co-op, but you won't have a business." Home healthcare isn't an easy business, he continued. "There's lots of investment in the workforce and the back office, billing and collecting properly, legal compliance. You have to have expertise."[11]

He emphasized that it's equally true that "we're much more than a business." When management restructures processes, "we think: what would be in the best interest of a home care worker?" Michael continued, "It's not that the workers run the place." Cofounder Rick Surpin was emphatic on that point. As he once put it, his vision is management that is "participatory" but not "collectivist."[12] (A *collective* is an organization managed without hierarchy in which every member has equal decision-making power.)

TRANSFORMING OWNERSHIP FROM EXTRACTION TO BELONGING

"It would be hard to take all these practices and put them in a publicly traded company," Michael said. CHCA was incubated by the nonprofit Community Service Society (CSS), where Rick worked, which sought to create jobs by forming worker-owned firms. CSS absorbed the early risk, then when the business was stable, transitioned it to worker ownership to ensure workers' interests remained top priority.[13]

Workers have a chance to build their skills, as 40 percent of administrative staff comes from the field. And as Adria said, "We have 300 workers trained as ambassadors, to go out into the community and talk about the co-op and why places should want to do business with us."[14]

Workers have various forms of voice, including voting for the board and serving on the labor-management committee, a key place to resolve conflict. But most important is the sense of community they feel. As cofounder Peggy put it, "It's about feeling like an outsider, and this place helps you feel like an insider."[15] In a book-length study of CHCA's culture done years ago by oral historians Ruth Glasser and Jeremy Brecher, staffer Betsy Smulyan told them that the sense of ownership CHCA aides feel comes less from having a vote in governance than from informal interactions—coming to the office, chatting with people. That lived sense of community is important in the isolating work of home care.[16]

At CHCA, in play is a subtle shift in the unconscious view of what a company is. In an investor-centered enterprise, firms are viewed as objects; that's the perspective of owners who stand apart from a firm, seeking to extract wealth from it. When owners stand *inside* a company doing its daily work, the nature of the firm is transformed: from object to community. Ownership is transformed from financial extraction to human belonging.

BUILDING A POWERFUL ECOSYSTEM FOR MISSION

A business seeking to maximize profit would have chosen a different niche in the home care market. CHCA primarily serves clients on Medicaid, who are the poor and persons with disabilities—not the most lucrative clients.

A central aim is good wages, but that's challenging. In 1997, CHCA prided itself on paying wages and benefits 10 to 20 percent higher than the industry norm—plus dividends of between $200 and $400 a year.[17] Then public funding for home healthcare was slashed 40 percent and one in five provider agencies closed. CHCA survived with anchor support from places like Visiting Nurse Service of New York (VNSNY). Because of CHCA's superior work, VNSNY—which accounted for 60 percent of the NYC market—was willing to pay more.[18]

CHCA also set out to shift the market itself. The company created Paraprofessional Healthcare Institute (PHI), a nonprofit policy and consulting arm that handles training for CHCA and has helped raise the wage floor for all home healthcare workers.[19] And CHCA founding president Rick Surpin left to launch a third organization, the nonprofit Independence Care System (ICS), a Medicaid managed long-term care plan serving adults with disabilities and the elderly, which by 2018 had grown into a massive $450 million enterprise. ICS over 20 years proved to be a major engine for CHCA's growth, contracting in 2018 for more than 1,100 CHCA aides. But in spring 2019, ICS began a major restructuring, closing down and reopening in a smaller new form—including a shift of CHCA clients to VNSNY. The long-term impact on CHCA is uncertain.[20]

Today the engine for growing this model is a movement to replicate CHCA, with 15 worker-owned home care agencies now in existence or in formation.[21] A leader of this movement is ICA Group, founded by Steve Dawson, which aided CHCA's launch through technical assistance and loans from what is now the Local Enterprise Assistance Fund. ICA has helped develop home health companies in five states. For three years, there's even been an annual conference for this movement—the National Home Care Cooperatives Conference—organized by the Cooperative Development Foundation.[22]

The possibilities for growth are immense. Home health aide jobs are projected to expand by 1 million by 2024. "Employee ownership has a unique value-add to the sector," David Hammer executive director of ICA Group told us, because the model creates competitive advantage through higher quality service and lower turnover. Worker cooperatives could dominate this niche, David believes—and Adria agrees.[23]

Private sector players tend to avoid low-profit sectors like this—as was true with rural electrification, where consumer-owned electric cooperatives now dominate. It's telling that the national conference for home care co-ops is held at a finance company owned by 900 rural electric co-ops. The size of this one lender—the National Rural Utilities Cooperative Finance Corporation—is greater than anyone might guess, with assets of $25 *billion*.[24] That hints at the scale possible when co-ops dominate in a niche.

THE RIGGED GAME OF WORK

Throughout this movement to make more CHCA-type companies, the shared aim is good work. That's an aim in contrast to the extractive economy that has been systematically expelling workers and worker income. Unemployment is reported as low—in 2018, around 4 percent in the US. Yet this figure only counts the jobless who've looked for work in the last *four weeks*. When the jobless-and-looking period is extended to a year—including part-time workers seeking full-time work—unemployment doubles to 8 percent.[25]

The *under*employed are vaster still. The Government Accountability Office, in a 2015 report, estimated that contingent workers—people getting by with temporary, part-time, self-employed, contract, or

Uber-economy–type employment—were a jaw-dropping *40 percent* of all workers.[26]

It's little wonder that in recent decades income has been rising slowly for the 117 million adults on the lower half of the income ladder.[27] The fruits of productivity have flowed to capital. The slice of GDP going to corporate profit doubled in recent decades—from 6 percent to 12 percent (see Figure 1).[28]

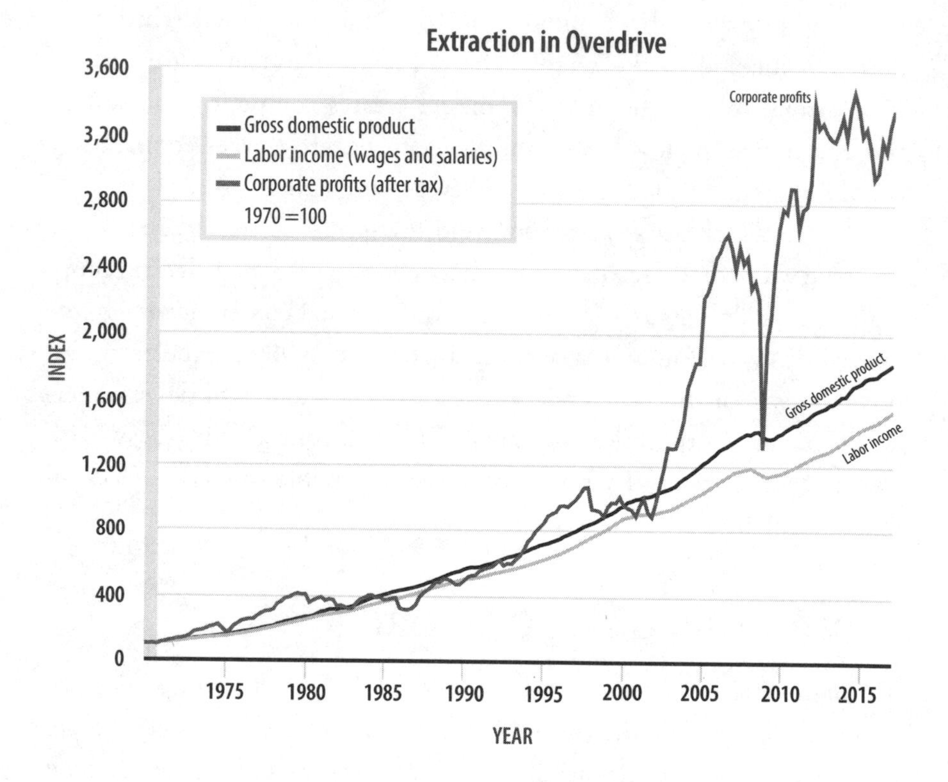

FIGURE 1. Corporate profits vs. GDP vs. labor income since 1970.[29] *The Index places the three trends on the same scale so that relative growth can be compared. (*SOURCE*: U.S. Bureau of Ecomomic Analysis)*

What's at work is the shattering of human lives. Among the many ailments suffered by the jobless are shortened life spans, demoralization, increased chronic disease, and opioid addiction. It's harder to recover from a period of joblessness than from the death of a loved one or a life-changing injury. Good work brings us not only income but a sense of identity, a feeling of self-worth, the energy from having a purpose, the sense of pride in playing a productive role in the community.[30]

In favoring capital over labor, our economy works against the well-being of most people. A key reason is our notion of ownership. The tenuous relationship shareholders have with public corporations—with shares held for minutes by those who do not know the names of "their" corporations—is dignified by the name *ownership*. Workers who go to a company every day, producing its wealth, are dispossessed.

An economy designed for the flourishing of all is an economy centered significantly on labor. It's a social order where labor deserves full membership in the economy, much as blacks and women won full membership in the polity. In the words of Thomas Paine, a key principle of democracy has to do with the common person and "whether the fruits of his labor shall be enjoyed by himself." Paine's vision was of "every man a proprietor." The modern equivalent is every employee an owner.[31]

Asset ownership is foundational to creating a worker-centered economy. As the CHCA ecosystem shows, other approaches are also needed, including minimum wage increases, unions, policy protections, and anchor institution support.

LABOR AS A COST TO BE ELIMINATED

Most basic is shifting our mindset about the nature of labor. British coal economist E. F. Schumacher, in his seminal 1973 essay, "Buddhist Economics," invited us to challenge the assumptions we hold unconsciously about work and workers. We tend to view work as a necessary evil, he said. For employers, it's "simply an item of cost, to be reduced to a minimum if it cannot be eliminated altogether, say, by automation." From the point of view of workers, work is unpleasant, to be undertaken grudgingly, with leisure vastly preferred. "Hence the ideal from the point of view of the employer is to have output without employees, and the ideal from the point of view of the employee is to have income without employment."[32]

In a capital-centered economy, superior persons are those who possess capital, leaving them free from labor, while those forced to labor are socially inferior. Schumacher offered a corrective, observing that work potentially enlivens our highest selves, allowing us to produce the best we are capable of. To organize work so that it becomes "meaningless, boring, stultifying" for the worker, Schumacher argued, is "little short of criminal."[33]

Work as a way of developing human capabilities is what CHCA is about. "I've often felt invisible and I feel that most people who are born working class feel invisible," cofounder Rick Surpin once said. With CHCA, the aim was to create a place "where invisible people can feel visible and valued."[34]

Building such empowerment in a workplace is complex. CHCA cofounders acknowledged the inevitable tension between running a viable business and realizing cultural ideals. Peggy recalled that, in the early days, "we painted this picture like everybody was equal," and then when managers exercised their power, "we began to be distrusted as being hypocritical."[35]

Having equal dignity in an employment situation doesn't mean there are no managers. Workers don't vote on all decisions, any more than citizens in a city vote on which streets are paved. Any social order—a city, a nation, a workplace—requires competent management, selected based on skills and empowered to perform their jobs.

The genius of CHCA seems to lie less in worker voting power than in democratic purpose. This company places at the center of its concern the creation of good work, good lives, for low-income black women, Latina women, immigrant women. In the words of our colleague Ronnie Galvin, vice president of engaged practice at The Democracy Collaborative, "If we don't have a movement that is fiercely centered on the reality" of such women—those who stand at the intersection of bias based on gender, race, and class—"then we will tinker at the margins" of the system. When we center our work on the most marginalized, he wrote, we can trust that this means "we all win."[36]

THE FIGHT OF OUR LIVES

Today CHCA is battling converging headwinds, even as it works to turn around a decline in worker-owners from prior years. Becoming an owner requires payment of $1,000, with most paying $50 upfront and the rest through weekly payroll deductions of $3.65. Workers get the $1,000 back when they leave, meanwhile potentially receiving annual dividends. But in four recent years, no dividend could be paid. On top of that, CHCA onboarded hundreds of workers from other agencies, with CHCA staff not always having time to educate them about ownership. From a high of 70 percent in 2007, the number of worker-owners dropped below 50 percent.

But that number has been rising for two years, Adria said. In 2017 and 2018 CHCA paid dividends, and 2017's was a record high at $800 for the average worker. The number of worker-owners has now rebounded from a low of 850 to 1,100. "We went to human resources and said, this is part of our roots, we need to get back to this," Adria emphasized. She added that the new organization Certified Employee-Owned (Certified EO)—which offers certification and branding for employee-owned companies—was also an "incredible" help in developing marketing materials for workers inside CHCA.[37]

This year, 2019, the new mandated minimum wage for New York state kicked in, at $15 an hour. Reimbursement rates are not keeping pace, making cash flow a major challenge. Medicaid rates factor in the wage increase, but managed long-term care plans don't necessarily pass that entire increase on to providers like CHCA, Adria said. CHCA can end up short on each hour. "With 3 to 5 million hours, every nickel, you feel it," she said.[38] Other high-road employers and CHCA are working with Service Employees International Union (SEIU) Local 1199 on solutions, like ensuring full compliance by care plans. "For those of us organized by 1199, the union makes sure the legislation is carried out," Adria said. "But not every organization has 1199."[39]

Meanwhile, there's also the restructuring of ICS and the uncertainties it leaves in the air. "We're in the fight of our lives," Adria told us. The year 2019 will be pivotal. Yet as she put it, "We're ready to do what it takes to be here at least the next 30 years."[40]

6

THE PRINCIPLE OF DEMOCRATIC OWNERSHIP

CREATING ENTERPRISE DESIGNS FOR A NEW ERA

The employee-owned benefit corporation, EA Engineering

Capitalism and business are, after all, virtually synonymous—capitalism being the historian's term for the system abstractly conceived, business the common word for the system in its daily operation.... Capitalism will inevitably change, and in the longer run will gradually give way to a very different kind of social order.

—ROBERT HEILBRONER, 1965[1]

We are people using business as a force for good... Certified B Corporations are a new kind of business that balances purpose and profit.

—B CORPORATION WEBSITE, 2018

"These are retirement fish," Mike Chanov said, pointing to a half-dozen spotted, six-inch fish in a tank, swimming lazily around a fake green palm. "Rainbow trout is one of the more sensitive species," he explained. These fish survived the tests this water quality lab put them through and have been put out to pasture, so to speak, as retirees.[2]

Mike gestured around the water lab—a low, white warehouse of a building, adjacent to the headquarters of EA Engineering, Science, and Technology, Inc., PBC, the environmental consulting firm in Hunt Valley, Maryland, that runs this ecotoxicology lab. "We raise testing species," he continued, pointing to eight shallow, round dishes, each holding a dozen or so water fleas. "All the water fleas are under 24 hours old," he said, all clones of each other. If the fleas fail to reproduce, that's an indicator of toxic water quality.

Mike showed us other species—Kevin the crab, fathead minnows, Atlantic purple urchins. The latter are richly hued, spiny creatures in a plastic bin the size of a brownie pan. "They'll be exposed to distillery effluent and will have to be euthanized," Mike said. We began to understand the trout's good fortune.

As EA Engineering (EA) tests water samples on these organisms, it's looking for violations of regulatory limits. These can be costly; a Maryland power plant operator recently paid $2 million for fines and upgrades to wastewater treatment facilities.[3] The lab runs 1,500 tests annually, just one part of the expansive work of EA, which has more than 500 employees and revenue of $140 million.

The far-flung work of this company has included testing low-maintenance ways to reduce erosion in stream banks in Guam using native plants and grasses; doing a stream flow study for a municipal power plant in West Virginia looking at impacts on fish; and cleaning up a shuttered defense site at Lake Ontario once used for manufacturing chemical warfare materials. As its mission statement says, EA Engineering is in the business of "improving the quality of the environment, one project at time."

EA Engineering is a profit-making company. Yet it's out to balance purpose with profit, not to maximize profits at all costs. That, they've discovered, makes all the difference.

This enterprise is a rare creature that has experienced both extractive and democratic ownership and lived to tell the tale—escaping, like the retiree fish, into a more humane existence. Today it's 100 percent employee-owned. And it's incorporated as a public benefit corporation (the "PBC" after "Inc." in its name), which means its core mission is to benefit society, not just company owners.

EA embodies the *principle of democratic ownership*, where enterprises have a designed-in commitment to the common good, with asset ownership broadly held by ordinary people. It's a harbinger of enterprise design for a new era of equity and sustainability. How EA found its way to this design is instructive.

A COSTLY DETOUR THROUGH NASDAQ

In the minds of many entrepreneurs, the chance to take a company public, with shares trading on a public stock exchange, represents the ultimate dream come true. For EA founder Loren Jensen, that dream proved a nightmare.

Loren is a limnologist, a scientist studying fresh water bodies such as wetlands and lakes, who at one point was mentored by Rachel Carson. In the early 1970s, when the Environmental Protection Agency was created and the Clean Water Act passed, Loren was a professor at Johns Hopkins University. He began consulting with companies. In 1973, he left the university to start a consulting firm, initially named Ecological Analysts, with a staff of aquatic biologists. It was one of the first firms to approach environmental work from a scientific perspective rather than an engineering perspective.

"We went into business with a half-dozen good clients, and in a few years, we had 70 or 80," Loren, now retired, recalled in a Skype interview. "We were being encouraged to go national. To do that, we needed capital." All of the firm's advisers encouraged Loren to take it public.[4]

He did so in 1986, and through the 1990s, the company's shares traded on NASDAQ. Initial success gave way to tumult, as EA cycled through three presidents, watched staff morale plummet, and found itself in trouble with the Securities and Exchange Commission over accounting misstatements.

Outside executives had been brought in, intent on pleasing Wall Street. They were "Enron kind of guys," senior scientist Bill Rue told us, as we sat in a small conference room at EA headquarters—in a LEED-certified Platinum building (Leadership in Energy and Environmental Design is a green building certification; Platinum is its highest level). As he spoke, Bill sipped from a compostable plastic cup. "A lot of the family atmosphere disappeared," he continued.[5] Numbers had to be hit. Quality work and integrity took a back seat to share price.

At a conference one day, Loren invited Bill for a walk and asked him, "What do you think of how things are going?" "I didn't feel comfortable, but I told him that [this executive] wasn't looking out for the company as a whole, he was looking out for himself," Bill recalled. Three weeks later, that executive was gone.

Loren bought back controlling interest with a minority partner. The outside executives were expunged. Their approach, current President Ian MacFarlane told us, was incompatible with the firm's environmental mission, which "couldn't be cooked into quarterly earnings." That was 2001.[6]

BUYING BACK SANITY

Late in 2001, the Enron scandal broke. Countless firms—Enron, Tyco, WorldCom, Adelphia, and Arthur Andersen in the US, Parmalat in Europe, and others—were discovered cooking the books to keep share prices aloft. Amoral leadership stood revealed as alarmingly pervasive in the extractive economy.

"Shareholders are only looking to get rich," Loren told us. "I don't mean to disparage capitalism, but the reality is, nobody buys stock except in the hope of a good return on investment. The problem this poses for a company like EA is you confuse and compromise corporate goals. It was very difficult to manage in that environment."

As Loren spoke over Skype, he came across as a plain-spoken, no-nonsense person—like a kind uncle. One value Loren instilled was "prudence," Ian said. "Prudence is decidedly Loren. Who has that in the core values of their company? We give money back to our clients if we don't use it all." EA had always focused on client intimacy, on protecting ecosystem health, a sensibility that clashed with the go-go culture of the stock market.

"My sense is the years we spent in the public markets were educational, but only in the sense that a horsewhipping is educational," Loren said. "We returned immediately to the task of understanding environmental problems and knowing what to do about them."

Loren brought in his son-in-law, Peter Ney, as chief financial officer (later named a "Top CFO" by *Baltimore Business Journal*).[7] He and Ian led a buyout of Loren and his minority partner, transitioning to full ownership by an employee stock ownership plan (ESOP) in 2014. At the same time, they rechartered the firm in Delaware as a PBC, declaring a binding commitment to balance purpose with profit.

Ian had learned about the benefit corporation idea at a nephew's wedding in 2012, in conversation with a guest, Christina Forwood. She works at B Lab, the nonprofit that developed the concept and worked to enact it in 34 states. "I said to myself, wouldn't this be cool to consider," Ian recalled. Peter saw an ESOP as good fit with Loren's goal of preserving his legacy and the company culture.

The two design elements—employee ownership and a purpose of public benefit—meshed perfectly. Bringing control into the hands of mission-oriented owners empowered EA to restore its identity and financial health. Through the ESOP, the company used its financial strength to buy out the founder, Peter explained. "We were already doing things that were ESOP-like, so it was no change at all," Ian added.[8]

EA has been profitable ever since. Legal and related costs for the new design were $750,000, but that "was much less than one year's savings in taxes," Peter said. As an S Corporation fully owned by an ESOP trust, EA pays zero income tax on profits at the enterprise level. Profits are passed through to employees, who pay taxes when they retire and withdraw holdings, when they're in a lower tax bracket.

Loren got additional personal tax advantages for selling to the ESOP. Employees received their shares for free, as a retirement benefit (unlike a worker cooperative, where workers buy their shares). As share price advances, employees gain more; in the first 12 years of the ESOP, share price quadrupled (this too differs from a worker co-op, where share price stays the same). Bill Rue, the senior scientist, with EA for more than 38 years, told us he had six figures in his retirement account. No individual today holds more than 5 percent of ownership.

A CATALYST FOR EMPLOYEE INVOLVEMENT

"We all feel more equal" with employee ownership, Bill said. "But it's not employee-controlled," added Barb Roeper, senior engineer, also there in the room with us. "People would love to have more say, but it can become unwieldy," she continued. As with many ESOPs, employee-owners at EA do not vote for board seats (in worker co-ops, by contrast, all employee-owners have a vote). An ESOP trustee is generally appointed by management. EA does, however, pass through more voting to employees on major decisions than the law requires, Ian explained.

Under the old Enron-style leaders, arbitrary layoffs were made, Barb said. "Now we have a policy of openness," she continued. "It's become more participatory. Millennials want more of that." There are more committees, plus soliciting of employee feedback. EA also practices open book management, sharing financial information.

On the day we visited, we sat in on an "all-hands" meeting, where Mike Battle, chief operating officer, discussed revenue and profits, including "66 consecutive quarters of profitability." He talked about sources of company contracts, the ESOP, paid time for volunteering, new green composting bins, company donations to Water for People, how one employee would go to Guatemala to observe that nonprofit in action. Bruce Muchmore was celebrated for joining the 40-year club of those with four decades at EA.

Afterward we asked young analyst Erin Toothaker whether she thought of herself as an owner. "When I think about my ownership of EA, I think about how I align myself with what we want to accomplish, rather than with a dollar holding in the company" Erin said. She said being a public benefit corporation was a "huge part of our strategic plan."

"One of the big things ESOPs wrestle with is employee engagement," Peter said. Some solve that by creating a board governance role for all levels of staff. "We could never do that and actually survive," Ian said. Peter added, "In our industry, the biggest thing that drives our employees is improving the environment." He said if you stopped an employee in the hall and asked: Would you rather help to clean up a site or be part of board discussions about risk? Ian broke in, "Oh my God, they would much prefer to do what our mission has us do."

Ian said being a public benefit corporation had been a catalyst for employee involvement, helping the firm sort out its corporate social responsibility (CSR) ethic. Public benefit incorporation is "CSR on steroids," he said. EA from the start was about multiple stakeholders—government entities, corporate clients, the ecosystem. "You've got to look at the whole system," Ian said. Because ecosystems are inherently long term and multistakeholder, enterprise design must be the same.

COMPANIES AS LIVING SYSTEMS

If the arc of EA's ownership shift may be esoteric to many people, it offers vital design lessons for the journey to a democratic economy. In the extractive economy, companies are seen as objects owned by shareholders, designed to manufacture earnings like so many ball bearings off an assembly line. EA is a model of a company as a living system, part of the larger living system of the earth, designed to benefit life.

EA Engineering's story illustrates the fork in the road that founders face. No founder lives forever, and few firms survive in family ownership beyond the second generation. A choice arises: to transition to financially oriented ownership or maintain the founding legacy through mission-oriented ownership. Most founders don't realize there is a choice, so strong are the forces pushing toward a purely financial sale. In the case of EA, *all* the company's advisers urged it to go public.

✦ ✦ ✦

But new models are arising, showing what enterprise design for a sustainable and equitable era can look like. Both EA Engineering and Cooperative Home Care Associates are employee-owned benefit corporations. Both have public benefit as their core mission, along with broad-based ownership. It's a design that empowers ethical leadership.

It's a starting framework of enterprise design for the 21st century and beyond. At The Democracy Collaborative, we've found more than 50 enterprises that are employee-owned benefit firms and B Corporations, including Eileen Fisher, New Belgium Brewing, Gardener's Supply, South Mountain Company, King Arthur Flour, and Namaste Solar. These companies pair a mission of serving the public good with ownership broadly held. In short, they're models of democratic ownership.

BEYOND THE BUSINESS CASE

Most of us don't realize ownership has a design. We think of ownership as a fact: you own something or you don't. The sustainability community, in particular, has ignored the issue of ownership, says UK sustainability consultant Carina Millstone. While the environmental movement has focused on physical technologies, it's neglected the more fundamental question of the ownership designs driving corporate decisions—and the question of which ownership designs are more supportive of ethical, sustainable decisions.

Environmental advocates tend to make the "business case" for sustainability, emphasizing reputation, risk, cost savings, and brand positioning. But Millstone points to an eight-year study by Massachusetts Institute of Technology and Boston Consulting Group, which found that only 37 percent of firms had discovered how to reap financial rewards for sustainability steps.[9]

Millstone says sustainability cannot be driven by purely commercial concerns. It requires *moral decision making*. When investors and executives are laser focused on maximum financial gain, sustainability investments can only be justified when they yield short-term profits. That's particularly true with publicly traded companies, where shareholders are large in number, geographically remote, disengaged, and structurally limited in their ability to effectively voice social and ecological responsibility. It's not a design for moral leadership. For owners to become moral agents, Millstone argues, companies need shareholders that are fewer in number, close to the firm, engaged, and committed to a common social or environmental mission.[10]

Sustainability rests on the ethical notion that we have a responsibility to others, those living today and in the future. Extractive design relies on the principle of shareholder primacy, which dates to the 1919 Michigan Supreme Court case, *Dodge v. Ford*, which said directors are to operate a company to benefit shareholders, not workers or customers. That premise, a living fossil of the Model T era, is a century old this year. Ours is a different time. It's an era, as Millstone writes, when "[p]rivate-sector firms have helped bring the Planet to its knees."

WHY EXTERNAL REGULATION ISN'T ENOUGH

Ownership design will shape our future fate—as it shaped the fate of Toms River, New Jersey, where the chemical company Ciba-Geigy and its predecessor firms made a home for 30 years, and where EA Engineering and its water testing once made a walk-on appearance. It's a tale that tells us about the difficulty of trying to regulate companies externally, while leaving their profit-maximizing DNA untouched.

The chemical industry came to Toms River in the 1950s, and in the following three decades the town suffered a poisoned town water supply, toxic backyard wells, and dozens of childhood cancers, "far too many to be coincidence," wrote Dan Fagin in his Pulitzer Prize-winning book, *Toms River*. In this community, EA was retained at some point—as Bill Rue put it in an email—"to conduct a dye dilution study of wastewater being discharged to the Atlantic."[11]

The wastewater in question was the 5 million gallons, *per day*, of highly acidic, partially treated toxic waste that Ciba-Geigy dumped into the ocean for 20 years. It was waste from synthetic dye manufacture—as Fagin wrote, "a phenomenally profitable business, as long as no one paid too much attention to what the manufacturing process left behind." Only when the US Superfund law was passed in 1980 did toxic waste become of serious corporate concern, because it became a substantial liability on balance sheets.[12]

Ciba-Geigy's continued ability to do ocean dumping now hinged on water testing. In 1982, when wastewater was tested on tiny mysid shrimp, more than half died. Later, water testing discovered toxins in backyard wells near a leaking company pipeline. So after 34 years, when it had dumped an estimated *40 billion gallons* of wastewater into the Atlantic, Ciba-Geigy threw in the towel.[13] Like many chemical companies at that time, it moved production to places like Alabama, Louisiana, and Asia, where wages and environmental oversight were much lower.[14]

Regulation didn't solve the problem of toxic pollution. Ciba-Geigy addressed the only problem it cared about, which was financial liability. That alone was material. The possible death of millions of ocean creatures—for whom the mysid shrimp had been tiny stand-ins—was not material. Since ocean creatures are not assets of a chemical corporation, the company believed it had no fiduciary duty to protect them, or the residents of Toms River.

This is not a view the planet can long survive. That it remains the view of globe-spanning multinationals—which have become like private governments, as Franklin Roosevelt observed—goes to the heart of today's crises.[15] Regulations at odds with corporate purpose are seen by companies mostly as nuisances they seek to shed. The public good needs to penetrate the DNA of enterprise.

It's no accident that Ian MacFarlane is a trustee of the Greenleaf Center for Servant Leadership. As the center's website says, the servant-leader "puts the needs of others first."[16] This kind of moral leadership is made possible by democratic ownership design.

✦ ✦ ✦

The innovative ownership design of EA Engineering is a promising emerging model. It has much to teach us about changing the DNA of larger corporations like Ciba-Geigy. But what's the route to getting there? One possible path is illustrated by the advance of LEED green building norms. What began as the visionary work of a few green architects and builders became a set of codified norms, over time enacted into law. New York City in 2005 required new buildings receiving city funding to meet LEED standards, and other cities following suit include Boston, Dallas, Kansas City, Los Angeles, and more. Pleasanton, California, requires LEED certification for all commercial construction over a certain size.[17]

Benefit corporations are themselves a form of codification, with requirements in state law, such as reporting publicly on social and environmental performance. Encouragement of ESOPs is already codified in the US in substantial tax incentives, and worker co-ops are designs in the law of many nations. One could envision such norms advancing to new stages, with government incentivizing and ultimately requiring a phase-in of democratic ownership. At the same time, we could prohibit extractive ownership in sectors like healthcare and education. At some point, society must redesign the operating system of major corporations. If we don't, democratic designs may remain forever marginal or face absorption.

First, we need to recognize ownership design matters. How many theorists worldwide today are working on ownership design, compared to the number working on climate change? How many business schools teach alternative forms of ownership? Abysmally few.

THE DEMOCRATIC ECONOMY MODEL READY FOR SCALE

Unlike the monoculture of extractive design, democratic design relies upon a diversity of public, private, cooperative, and employee-owned designs, structured at different scales and in different sectors to create the outcomes we seek. Among these models, employee ownership is the most ripe for going to scale.

Employee ownership is growing in the UK, and already widespread in the US, where there are 6,600 firms with some employee ownership. The average equity share of employee-owners in an ESOP is $134,000, according to Rutgers University employee-ownership expert Joseph Blasi—almost ten times the average retirement account for American households headed by someone between the ages of 55 and 64 ($14,500).[18]

Employee-owned companies are more resilient in times of economic stress, and worker-owners are one-fourth as likely to be laid off. The National Center for Employee Ownership in the US found that, among workers aged 28–34, those at employee-owned firms had nearly double the household net worth compared to other workers, plus they enjoyed 33 percent higher wage income.[19]

Retiring baby boom entrepreneurs are likely to sell or close 2.34 million businesses over the coming decade; many will simply shut down, resulting in layoffs and the loss of local jobs.[20] If these could be converted to employee ownership, it could bend the curve of history. To help advance this, we at The Democracy Collaborative created our Fifty by Fifty initiative, aimed at catalyzing 50 million employee owners by 2050.[21] There are also 6,000 benefit corporations—the vast majority still owned by founders. If more of these converted to employee ownership, to preserve mission, next generation enterprise design could be well on its way.

✦ ✦ ✦

"I've gotten even more radical since the last time we spoke," Ian said, when we talked after our visit. He spoke of the Academy of Management academic meeting he attends, where he's involved in a group on "critical management studies," examining all that's wrong with business management. Much of the focus is stakeholder management. For Ian, it's more than theory. "The combination of employee ownership and being a benefit corporation—if you get into that framework," Ian said, "you have new fiduciary duties." EA Engineering has a legally binding duty to create public benefit, and as the company's value grows, that wealth goes to employees.[22] The reason is simple but invisible: ownership design.

7

THE PRINCIPLE OF SUSTAINABILITY

PROTECTING THE ECOSYSTEM AS THE FOUNDATION OF LIFE

The Federal Reserve's power to finance ecological transition

The right of the people to use and enjoy air, water, and sunlight are essential to life, liberty, and the pursuit of happiness. These basic human rights have been impaired by those who discharge toxic substances into the air, water, and land. Contaminating the commons must be recognized as a fundamental wrong in our system of laws, just as defacing private property is wrong.[1]

—WINONA LADUKE

"I didn't want people to think I was this lone crazy woman from Brazil," Carla Santos Skandier said with a laugh, "when in fact I have this whole organization behind me." She was recalling the presentation she'd made to a group of environmental funders, some of whom didn't realize she was part of The Democracy Collaborative. But she needn't have worried. What Carla had to say, in her five-minute pitch, caused a stir in the room. "After the presentations, they gave each of us a table so people could follow up individually. My table was full from beginning to end," Carla said. "It seemed I had more than any other table. I had people coming before I even got there."[2]

The lead funders present that morning were on an urgent quest: "Ending the Age of Oil." They were part of the Climate Change Accelerator (later renamed the Climate Breakthrough Project), which was in search of breakthrough ideas—"novel and potentially game-changing strategies"—to dramatically cut carbon emissions over a decade. The project was an initiative of the David and Lucile Packard Foundation, in partnership with the Oak Foundation and the Good Energies Foundation. These and other funders had come to this breakfast meeting at The Battery in San Francisco on September 6, 2017, to hear from eight Oil Lab Fellows, selected out of more than 500 applications, from 89 countries. Carla was one of the eight. By the end of the day, she was one of three to receive funding.[3]

As people crowded Carla's table, they were coming to hear about a crazy idea: having the federal government buy out oil companies and wind them down, using the same technique the Federal Reserve used to bail out big banks in 2008: quantitative easing (QE)—conjuring money out of thin air, without a dime of cost to taxpayers.

Carla and The Democracy Collaborative's team at our Next System Project call this *QE for the planet.* Maybe not the sexiest moniker, but hey.

Funders that day took an unusual step in funding Carla. While they'd intended to fund only two ideas—ready to roll out—they made an exception for Carla. Her concept was so enormous and out of left field, they greeted it with both skepticism and hey-what-if enthusiasm. The Climate Strategies Accelerator Fund, wrote Walt Reid of Packard in an email, was "trying something different, and decided to create a matching grant opportunity for Carla," to support her team in developing the concept. If Carla could find $100,000, the CSA Fund would match it.

It took seven months, but Carla found that funding and got the match. This environmental attorney from Brazil—formerly with the Rio de Janeiro Environmental Protection Agency—set to work.

LARGE-SCALE SYSTEM DYNAMICS

Movement into a next economic system can't wait for the long, slow process of building community wealth. To create space for alternatives to flourish, we must confront huge and immediate issues like climate change. Building a democratic economy may begin at the local level, but it requires tackling large system dynamics as well.

The world has a dozen years to prevent global warming catastrophe, warned the October 2018 report from the United Nations Intergovernmental Panel on Climate Change (IPCC), speaking in more dire terms than earlier. Previous reports from the IPCC had focused on keeping global temperatures below 2 degrees Celsius warming over preindustrial levels, but this report focused on keeping warming under 1.5 degrees. On that one-half degree difference hangs the fate of millions of lives.[4] If the planet is to stop short of 1.5 degrees, carbon emissions must be slashed 45 percent by 2030 from 2010 levels, then crushed down to net zero by 2050. This requires a transformation in civilization for which "there is no documented historic precedent," the panel wrote.[5]

Every year through 2035, the IPCC said, the world must invest $2.4 trillion in clean energy. That's a sevenfold increase from the $333.5 billion that Bloomberg estimates was invested in renewable energy in 2017.[6]

We must also invest massively *less* in fossil fuels, winding them down nearly entirely. But nations are doing the reverse. According to Oil Change International, G20 governments and multilateral development banks from 2014 to 2016 invested more than three times as much in oil and gas as in renewables—paving the path to disaster.[7]

Oil companies blithely pretend it isn't so. ExxonMobil in early 2018 announced plans to increase output 25 percent and double its earnings by 2025.[8]

"Global Warming's Terrifying New Math," as a Bill McKibben article termed it, shows why this growth must not materialize. Writing in 2012, he used the previous threshold of 2 degrees of warming. (A 1.5-degree threshold makes the math even more terrifying.) If the planet is to stay within a 2-degree threshold, it must stay within a carbon budget of 565 gigatons. But "the fossil fuel we're currently planning to burn" (currently proven reserves) is 2,795 gigatons—*five times higher* than the carbon budget. That means 80 percent of reserves must stay in the ground. It's unburnable carbon. In financial terms, *stranded assets.*[9]

John Fullerton, a former managing director at JP Morgan who now runs the Capital Institute, calculated that those stranded assets, at current market value, add up to $20 trillion. Keeping that carbon in the ground means writing off $20 trillion in assets. "[W]e might well burn all that carbon, in which case investors will do fine," McKibben wrote. "But if we do, the planet will crater."

This is the extraordinary end game of the extractive economy, which in its infancy did not shrink from commodifying human beings, in its maturity did not blink at dumping billions of gallons of toxins into oceans, and now in its aging fullness contemplates causing irreversible damage to life on earth, and shrugs.

A NEW MOONSHOT

If there is to be a twist in the plot, it may be the Green New Deal. It's a legislative suite of government action akin to Franklin Roosevelt's New Deal in the 1930s, which is serving as a collective vehicle for thinking imaginatively about scaling this hurdle unprecedented in human history.

As Saikat Chakrabarti, Representative Ocasio-Cortez's chief of staff, put it, "It is sort of like the moonshot. When JFK [John F. Kennedy] said America was going to go to the moon, none of the things we needed to get to the moon at that point existed. But we tried and we did it. [The Green New Deal] touches everything—it's basically a massive system upgrade for the economy."[10]

The Green New Deal is at once a strategy for deep decarbonization, a jobs creator, an infrastructure bill, and a reconvening of the commons. It could be a massive demonstration project for a democratic economy operating within planetary boundaries. And it might potentially create the public mobilization needed, because it's not just about surviving climate change but about inspiring people to realize we all can thrive.

One United Nations official described the 1.5-degree report as "a deafening, piercing smoke alarm."[11] When a smoke alarm goes off, you don't keep doing what you were doing. Yet funders, nonprofits, and policymakers cling to the same established, incremental strategies. We need breakthroughs. The Green New Deal could be one. QE for the planet could be another; conversations about combining the two approaches are underway. A key contribution of QE for the planet is that it points toward the deep institutional changes required for a democratic economy—a flag marking the territory we must ultimately claim.

THE HEART OF THE MATTER: THE DESIGN OF OWNERSHIP

Buying out oil companies is a strategy targeted directly at the design of ownership and control of corporations in the extractive economy. With maximizing short-term gains for shareholders considered the immutable aim, most established strategies operate *within* this aim: tax carbon to drive corporate profit-making the right direction; persuade companies of the business case for sustainability; invest in renewables to make big returns for investors.

All fine steps. Yet these approaches demonstrate how little we even dream of challenging capital's seeming right to eternal, maximum wealth extraction. The legitimacy of this right is rarely questioned, much as the absolute power of the monarchy and aristocracy was not questioned, before the advent of democracy. In a previous book, Marjorie termed it *The Divine Right of Capital.*

This unalterable scheme can be altered, virtually overnight, by buying a controlling interest in oil companies like ExxonMobil, Chevon, and ConocoPhillips—then installing a new board and embedding a new purpose: wind down production to safeguard life on earth. What this concept demonstrates—even as a thought experiment—is how the *principle of sustainability* must move inside ownership design. It shows us what it means to make preserving the ecosystem a new first principle of our political economy.

Democratic economy design recognizes the rights of property but balances them with other rights, including the right to planetary flourishing. No one's property is taken away in a buyout. Indeed, such a move might be welcomed by shareholders, once they recognize company assets will become stranded.

FROM REGULATION TO TAKEOVER

A public takeover becomes a logical answer, when we recognize that regulation is likely to be subverted, as corporate power continues to dominate decision making through lobbying, uncontrolled political contributions, and regulatory agency capture. Publicly listed corporations are subject to Wall Street's first commandment: grow or die. This mandate—and the increasing carbon emissions it demands—is today in the driver's seat economically, politically, and ecologically.

What prevents rapid action on climate change is the grip that fossil fuel corporations have on politics. ExxonMobil's scientists decades ago understood climate science, yet the company publicly manufactured doubts. BP and other large European emitters have made substantial donations to prominent climate-deniers in US Senate elections. The Koch brothers—oil barons of Koch Industries—have donated at least $100 million directly to 84 groups denying climate change science since 1997, according to Greenpeace.[12] In the US 2018 midterm elections, Colorado activists for a proposal to limit fracking were outspent forty to one.[13] As Bill McKibben put it, environmentalists must "focus fire on the fossil fuel industry," to see if "its political power can be broken."[14]

A government buyout of fossil-fuel companies may seem radical, but the US has a long history of such actions in a crisis. With the 2008 financial crisis, Presidents George W. Bush and Barack Obama in effect nationalized AIG and General Motors. Ronald Reagan in 1984 seized 80 percent of shares in Continental Illinois National Bank and Trust Company, when it was failing. Dozens of firms were nationalized during World War II, to ensure war production needs were met. In World War I private railroads—crucial to the transportation of war materials—were taken over by Woodrow Wilson and operated by the government until 1920.

IF WE CAN BAIL OUT THE BIG BANKS, HOW ABOUT THE PLANET?

A federal buyout would not burden taxpayers if the Federal Reserve Bank infused new money through the monetary policy of quantitative easing. In such a method, funds are directly created by a central bank, which is one way big banks were bailed out in the 2008–2009 mortgage meltdown. Following that crisis—created by the reckless loans and investments of big financial players—central banks worldwide pumped the equivalent of $12.3 trillion of new money into the financial system, including around $3.5 trillion by the US Federal Reserve between late 2008 and 2014. By taking toxic assets off the hands of failing financial institutions, the Fed gave those firms and their investors a parachute for a soft landing.[15]

It's a bit like if you or I loaned a friend $10,000 and found him unable to pay, only to have a kindly uncle pay off the loan in full. This is how Uncle Sam made trillions of dollars available to aid capital—even as regular folks (many of them people of color) struggled under mortgages suddenly larger than the sinking value of their homes. No kindly uncle for us.

Around the world, the European Union and Japan have recently been operating QE programs. In 2017, the European Central Bank was injecting more than $60 billion into financial markets monthly; it ran a four-year QE program that ended in December 2018 (and was revived in March 2019).[16] Balance sheets at central banks today are five times precrisis levels. None of this is "paid for" through taxes or borrowing.[17] Moreover, dire predictions of runaway inflation have yet to materialize.

"It's not tax money," former Federal Reserve Chairman Ben Bernanke explained in one TV interview. "The banks have accounts with the Fed, much the same way that you have an account in a commercial bank. So, to lend to a bank, we simply use the computer to mark up the size of the account that they have with the Fed."[18]

That central banks can create new money is difficult for most people to grasp. But it's reality. That's not to say such power is limitless. Hyperinflation can set in, as well as other problems. You can't call on your uncle every day. But in times of necessity, and within limits, it can be done. It's done all the time.

Theorists and policymakers today—including the Labour Party's Jeremy Corbyn in the UK, Alexander Barkawi of the Council of Economic Policies in Switzerland, and experts at the International Institute for Sustainable Development—have been calling for "Green QE," in which monetary creation by governments directly finances green infrastructure.[19]

"Leading central bankers are increasingly clear that dealing with the financial risks of climate change is part of their job," wrote Barkawi in the *Financial Times*. "Making sure that monetary policy is pointing in the same direction is a logical and necessary next step."[20]

◆ ◆ ◆

What would it take to buy out major US oil and gas companies? At market value from mid-year 2018, purchasing 51 percent of the top 25 US publicly traded oil and gas companies would take around $700 billion.[21] Not a small sum. But over seven years, it's $100 billion a year, far from impossible. By comparison, the wars in Iraq and Afghanistan will have cost something in the range of $4–7 trillion, when future costs for veterans are included. Not to mention Trump's tax cut of $1.5 trillion.[22]

WHAT COUNTS AS A CRISIS?

If we know money creation is an option in a crisis, the question becomes this: What counts as a crisis? Potential losses by big banks—from their own reckless actions—now that's a disaster. Who can forget the indelible image of US Treasury Secretary Hank Paulson, former CEO of Goldman Sachs, on bended knee before House Speaker Nancy Pelosi in 2008, begging for a federal bailout of $700 billion.

How about a warning from climate scientists that we have twelve years to avert global calamity? Yawn. Click to the next story. Interesting how $700 billion is the ticket for both crises.

Plenty of technical questions remain about a fossil fuel buyout, and Carla's team is working on them. But the real question is what we value. Hank Paulson got his bailout in the blink of an eye—followed by far more. Central banks didn't dither about technicalities and inflation risk. They acted, because what they valued was at risk.

We don't yet extend this level of care to the natural world. Conservationist Aldo Leopold talked about why, in *A Sand County Almanac*, published in 1966, in an era when ecological concerns often went by the term "conservation." He wrote

> *Conservation is getting nowhere because it is incompatible with our Abrahamic concept of land. We abuse land because we regard it as a commodity belonging to us. When we see land as a community to which we belong, we may begin to use it with love and respect.... That land is a community is the basic concept of ecology, but that land is to be loved and respected is an extension of ethics.*[23]

All ethics rests on the premise "that the individual is a member of a community of interdependent parts," Leopold wrote. "The land ethic simply enlarges the boundaries of the community to include soils, waters, plants, and animals, or collectively, the land." The land ethic, he continued, changes humanity "from conqueror of the land-community to plain member and citizen of it."[24]

We lack such an ethic because we view land as property, a relationship that entails "privileges but not obligations," Leopold wrote. A privilege of extraction; no obligation to protect.[25] Indigenous communities embody a different relationship to the land. As Julian Brave NoiseCat, a member of the Canim Lake Band Tsq'escenemc in British Columbia observed, indigenous peoples do not view land and water as property, but as "sacred, living relatives, ancestors, places of origin."[26]

This principle became law in New Zealand, where the Whanganui Maori, after a 140-year legal battle, succeeded in having their ancestral Whanganui River win legal rights equal to a human being. As this was enacted in 2017, two guardians were created on behalf of the river, one from the crown, one from the iwi.[27]

In the same spirit, US Ojibway leader Walt Bresette helped lead a movement in the 1990s that drafted a proposed amendment to the US Constitution. He pointed out that concern for future generations was already in the Constitution, where the Preamble speaks of securing "the Blessings of Liberty to ourselves and our Posterity." Building on this, the proposed Seventh Generation Amendment reads:

> *The right of citizens of the U.S. to enjoy and use air, water, sunlight, and other renewable resources determined by the Congress to be common property shall not be impaired, nor shall such use impair their availability for use by the future generations.*[28]

This amendment, the New Zealand victory, QE for the planet—all of these are acts of imaginative excellence, envisioning how the wealth of the earth might be decolonized from corporate control. They're not about incrementally less harm, but making the sustaining of life a first principle.

AN ETHICAL ECONOMY IS A RESILIENT ECONOMY

Ethics and finance are bending toward one another these days, as the carbon bubble is making the climate crisis an economic crisis. In 2015, Citigroup estimated the value of stranded assets could exceed $100 trillion—massively more than the stranded assets of the housing bubble.[29] Mark Carney, governor of the Bank of England, calculated that of all global wealth, fully one-third is invested in "carbon-heavy" companies, including fossil fuel and many other industries.[30] If many of these assets turn out to be worthless, the damage could be volcanic.

According to Carbon Tracker, we have four years before demand for fossil fuels peaks, in the year 2023.[31] After coal reached its peak in 2014, four major US coal companies filed for bankruptcy in the following three years. Things unravel fast.[32] The energy sector plummeted 20 percent in 2018, even as the Standard & Poor's 500 Index was down just 6 percent.[33]

A fossil fuel wind-down is coming. Yet it's not coming fast enough. "Once climate change becomes a defining issue for financial stability, it may already be too late," warned Mark Carney.[34] If we hope the short-term mindset of finance will wake up in time, we're in trouble. The alternative is to act through government, protecting our common good first—knowing that in the not-so-long run, this will protect us all, including finance.

THE PENNY DROPS

When Carla made her pitch at The Battery in San Francisco, she encountered lots of skepticism and questions about QE for the planet. Will QE cause inflation? That's a topic that Gar Alperovitz, political economist and cofounder of The Democracy Collaborative, addresses. Gar, earlier a legislative director in the US House and Senate, dreamed up the idea of QE for the planet—"It was hatched in my living room," Gar said—while Carla has led in developing it. Would QE for the planet lead to inflation? Not given the level of real unemployment in the US, he said. The idea that "we're at a limit of productive capacity where prices have to go up, that's almost certainly wrong." Wealthy stock owners receiving the buyout won't go out and buy a lot more, triggering inflation, Gar said. They'll invest the money.

At first, people thought a government takeover of oil companies "was a silly idea," Carla said. "Now people seem somewhat comfortable with that." It could be because urgency is now greater; it could also be because Trump talked about nationalizing the coal industry (not to wind down fossil fuels but ostensibly to protect jobs).

✦ ✦ ✦

At the Beacon Hotel in Washington, DC, where Gar has always held court, we slid into a booth and asked Gar about all this. The deeper issue is getting the oil companies out of politics, he said. "There's a whole series of environmental issues they stand in the way of."[35]

What about trade and leakage issues; will the oil simply be produced somewhere else? His answer was the same. "The strategy is almost entirely *political* in nature, not economic." What stopped the Obama Administration's climate change legislation was powerful lobbying, mostly by Big Oil. The goal of the QE for the planet strategy is to get control of fossil fuel companies, "and thereby to stop the massive political opposition to doing the right thing on climate change."[36]

As for quantitative easing, he admitted it strikes people as odd. "Creating money out of nothing?" he said. "Then the penny drops: 'Yeah, we could do that.'"

8

THE PRINCIPLE OF ETHICAL FINANCE

INVESTING AND LENDING FOR PEOPLE AND PLACE

Banks and pension funds invest for local wealth in Preston, England

---

The power of a few to manage the economic life of the nation must be diffused among the many or be transferred to the public and its democratically responsible government.

—FRANKLIN ROOSEVELT

"After so many years, I find myself in the mainstream now. It's odd," said Matthew Brown, in his distinctive British accent. "I've always found being in the minority more fascinating."

Those days on the margin are receding rapidly for Matthew, a city council member since 2002 in Preston, England, who in 2018 was elected leader of the council and now travels the country to talk about all that he's stirred up there. Matthew until recently worked a part-time government clerical job in addition to his Council work, spending evenings studying books on left-wing economics. As one reporter wrote, Matthew is a guy often seen with shoelaces untied, someone who grew up feeling "a sense of not being good enough," as he put it. These days Matthew is featured in places like The Economist *and* The Times *of London and serves as an adviser to the national Labour Party—which is itself experiencing an unexpected, swelling popularity. Labour might well form the next UK government. Some 60 cities and counties around the UK have reached out to Matthew—"too many to count," he said—and at least 10 cities are actively replicating some of the work he helped lead in his own city: a multifaceted approach to building community wealth that has come to be known as the "Preston Model."*[1]

The turning point for Preston was 2011. That was when a large corporation pulled out of the massive Tithebarn shopping mall project, spelling the death knell for what had been the Council's decade-long revitalization strategy. This high-poverty city was bereft: no money, no faith in a failing system, no plan. As the Council searched for ideas, Matthew heard about Ted, through Gordon Benson at the Centre for Local Economic Strategies (CLES). Out of the blue, Ted got a call out from this place he'd never heard of, Preston, asking him to come over. "It was amazing what they were doing in Cleveland," Matthew said, speaking of the employee-owned Evergreen cooperatives supported by anchor institutions. "I was shocked that people in America were looking at that model, because I thought they would see it as too socialist. We decided to adapt it for a UK setting."[2]

Although inspired by Cleveland, Preston ended up going far beyond Cleveland. Abandoning the idea of an absentee corporation as savior, Preston began cultivating locally owned firms. It started with Council support for creation of the Preston Cooperative Development Network, in partnership with the University of Central Lancashire. In 2012, Preston declared itself a living wage employer. The city also became an energy supplier by partnering with the municipal supplier Fairerpower Red Rose, saving consumers more than £2 million. The county pension fund—whose committee included the late Preston council leader Peter Rankin—allocated £150 million to local investment, including Preston projects like student housing and refurbishment of the once-grand Park Hotel.[3]

Most powerfully, Matthew worked with CLES on anchor institution spending, work which CLES had done previously in Manchester. CLES and the Preston Council identified £1 billion in anchor spending in 2012–2013, only 5 percent of which was spent locally. The Council sat down with six leading anchors—including the public housing authority, the University of Central Lancashire, and the local police authority—and persuaded them to buy more from Preston-based enterprises, such as farmers, printers, and construction firms. By 2016–2017, that 5 percent had grown to 18 percent in Preston, an increase of £75 million. Across the county of Lancashire, where Preston is located, anchor spending went from 39 to 79 percent, an increase of £200 million. This shift supported 4,500 jobs.[4]

The results have been remarkable. From 2016 to 2017, jobs in Preston paying less than a living wage dropped from 23 percent to 19 percent. Unemployment fell from 6.5 percent in 2014 to 3.1 percent. A 2018 study by PricewaterhouseCoopers and the London-based think tank Demos named Preston the most improved city in the UK and a better place to live than London. As Matthew said, the city had become more resilient by putting "more democracy and ownership in the Preston economy."[5]

The trailblazer for much of this was Matthew. "For a long time, he will tell you that he was pretty much a lone voice," Aditya Chakrabortty, senior economic commentator for *The Guardian*, told filmmaker Laura Flanders. "This isn't a model out of a textbook," he added. "It's experiments. It's things dreamt up in front of a laptop in the small hours of the morning with people thinking, what if I tried this idea."[6]

ENERGIZING THE ELECTORATE

Matthew and his once-marginal ideas in Preston are now at the epicenter of a sea change in the political dialogue in Britain. Matthew was tapped by Labour leader Jeremy Corbyn to serve on a new Community Wealth Building unit in the party. *The Economist* dubbed Preston "Jeremy Corbyn's Model Town."[7]

In a manifesto for the 2017 general election, Labour laid out a transformative agenda for broadening ownership and remaking the economy "for the many, not the few," Labour's new slogan. Although "Britain is a long-established democracy," the manifesto said, "the distribution of ownership of the country's economy means that decisions about our economy are often made by a narrow elite." The agenda included plans for protecting small business, growing worker-owned businesses, banning fracking, investing in renewable energy, and funneling support to local economies. In 2018, Labour announced a proposal to require all companies employing more than 250 to create worker ownership funds, giving workers a financial stake in their companies.[8]

Labour's plans also call for public ownership of the railways, energy, water, and the Royal Mail. As economic advisor John McDonnell emphasized, these new publicly owned companies would be more democratic than old-style nationalized industries that were often "too bureaucratic and too removed from the reality" of workers. Support for public ownership in the UK is overwhelmingly positive, with 83 percent favoring publicly owned water, 77 percent publicly run energy, and 60 percent publicly owned railways.[9]

Although Labour didn't win in 2017, it picked up an unexpected 40 percent of the vote, marginally behind the governing Conservative Party at 42 percent, despite what *The Guardian* termed a "thunderously hostile media." As one Labour member of Parliament put it, "A lot of people were saying they were frightened of the future and wanted an alternative."[10]

Labour's national agenda, combined with Matthew's local work, paints a picture of an emerging alternative system—capable of energizing a sizable electorate. There are lessons here about the surprising possibility of building real political power around a democratic economy agenda.

Beyond politics, another large-scale system dynamic at work in Preston and the UK is the power of finance. If climate change urges us toward a new sensibility—the ethical notion we have a responsibility to others, those alive today and in the future—finance in the extractive economy isn't there yet. Implicitly, it's built on the notion that finance dwells somehow in a realm apart, its rational workings removed from societal and ecological impacts, which need be considered only to the extent that capital is affected.

The democratic economy counterpoint is uncomplicated. It's the *principle of ethical finance*: banking and finance exist to serve people and planet, with profit the result and not the primary aim. We can see this principle emerging in Preston, which is a kind of microcosm for the extractive economy's long history, in which capital began as servant and ended up master—and is beginning, in small ways, to return to its true purpose.

A FATE BOUND UP WITH FINANCE

Preston in many ways was the birthplace of the Industrial Revolution—a cotton town where Richard Arkwright first created the spinning frame. As merchants in this rising new economy shipped materials, they obtained insurance from places like Edward Lloyd's Coffeehouse, which would become Lloyd's of London. Textiles and manufacturing helped make Preston a thriving mill town. But over the most recent half-century, capital and industry began to abandon Preston, as they did Cleveland.

The 2008 crash starkly demonstrated how intertwined Preston's fortunes had become with the big London banks. Deregulation in the 1980s resulted in the UK having one of the most centralized banking systems in the developed world, with five large shareholder-owned banks controlling an astonishing 90 percent of the market. As these banks swallowed up local banks and once–mutually owned building societies, bank lending to the real economy—like locally owned businesses in Preston—shriveled. Today that amounts to less than 10 percent of total lending. The rest shifted to such areas as insurance and pension funds, consumer finance, and commercial real estate—and to such speculative areas as securitization, where loans are sliced and diced and sold.[11]

The 2008 implosion of those toxic financial products stopped building cranes dead across Britain. That spelled the end to the Tithebarn project in Preston's city center. Although big banks were bailed out, Preston and other communities suffered through close to a decade of austerity due to shrinking aid from Westminster. By 2010, this town of 140,000 was near the bottom of the UK in terms of employment and well-being, with one in three children living in poverty. The birthplace of the Industrial Revolution had a new label, "the suicide capital of England."[12]

As Preston began to take back its fate from the impersonal global forces of the extractive economy, one Council strategy was to rebuild local banking. "In my ward, the last branch of a major bank is shutting down," Matthew said. This is typical of towns across Britain, where 762 bank branches were closed in 2017 alone.[13] The Council supported CLEVR, a credit union owned by and run on behalf of its members, as well as a local community-oriented financial institution, Moneyline. That entity—which is national yet rooted in the communities it serves—operates as an alternative to predatory payday lenders, offering flexible, affordable short-term loans, with no additional fees for late or missed payments. These institutions aim to serve their clients, not to extract maximum profits from them.

The Preston City Council is also studying two new banking models being built in the UK, Hampshire Community Bank and the Community Savings Banking Association. The Council hired an expert to study both and to make a recommendation to Lancashire leaders in 2019. "Then anchors like the university can decide if they want to invest," Matthew said. Hampshire Community Bank is modeled on Germany's local public savings and cooperative banks (Sparkasse and Volksbank). Sparkasse—by law chartered to support their communities—control just 30 percent of bank assets yet do 70 percent of lending to small- and medium-sized enterprises.[14]

The UK's Community Savings Banking Association, established in 2015 under the leadership of James Moore, aims to establish a network of 18 regional cooperative banks, each with a mission of local service. The banks will be controlled by customers, one member, one vote. The larger network will provide back office functions and regulatory support—essentially, a "bank in a box."[15]

One of the first of these regional banks is Avon Mutual. Jules Peck, its founding director—also a research fellow with The Democracy Collaborative—explained the new local banking movement this way: "These new regionally focused, mission-led community banks are set to disrupt the banking sector and put sustainable development, people and planet, back at the heart of the UK investment sector."[16]

BUILDING LOCALLY, SUPPORTING NATIONALLY

Preston has acted largely on its own while under siege, facing both austerity from the national government and the flight of capital from banks. The city will ultimately need national policy support. This is a key lesson for building a democratic economy: ventures can and often do begin at the local level. But to get to scale, government policies, particularly national ones, will be needed.

Labour has floated a variety of plans for creating a financial system beneficial to the real economy—including a proposed UK Investment Bank, modeled on other successful development banks like KfW in Germany. With assets of more than €500 billion, KfW played a countercyclical role in Germany during the financial crisis, increasing business lending 40 percent between 2007 and 2011, even as UK banks pulled back lending. KfW has special programs for small- and medium-sized businesses. It functions alongside the nation's extensive network of regional and savings banks to create a diverse, locally rooted, healthy banking ecosystem.[17]

The US has something similar in the Bank of North Dakota, owned by the state. It supports a network of locally owned banks and credit unions, and as a result, North Dakota has close to six times as many local financial institutions per capita as the US overall. Because of this banking system, North Dakota made its way through the 2008 recession unscathed—inspiring a rising movement to consider publicly owned banks in places such as New York City, Los Angeles, San Francisco, St. Louis, New Mexico, and New Jersey.[18]

CENTRALIZED EXTRACTION VERSUS A NETWORK OF LOCAL FLOWS

At work are two ways of thinking about why finance exists. In the extractive economy, the aim is maximum financial income for an elite, which means wealth is often siphoned from communities by the absentee City of London or Wall Street.

Democratic economy finance design is closer to the vision of author and activist Jane Jacobs, who wrote about feeding widespread flourishing through dispersed local flows. Jacobs led the successful movement in New York City that saved Greenwich Village from the wrecking ball of master builder Robert Moses. In his modernist mindset, Moses envisioned a 10-lane superhighway soaring above the city, the construction of which would have leveled dense city blocks that had thrived since the Dutch settled Manhattan centuries earlier. Jacobs and her ragtag band of localists improbably stopped that highway. She wrote of expressway construction: "This is not the rebuilding of cities. This is the sacking of cities."[19]

In a later book, *The Nature of Economies,* Jacobs observed that economic vitality depends upon enabling flows of energy throughout a system. Moses's vision—like that of the big banks—can be likened to a single concrete channel feeding an absentee community, while Jacob's vision is of a river fed by numberless tiny streams, enriching an entire landscape as it meanders through. One approach may be more efficient—for the narrow purposes of a particular group. The other is more resilient for the system overall.[20]

FINANCIALIZATION AND COLLAPSE

The extractive approach has been operating, full bore, in recent decades, leading to the phenomenon scholars call *financialization.* Author Kevin Phillips describes it as a process of financial services taking over "the dominant economic, cultural, and political role in a national economy." Financial deregulation under Reagan and Thatcher in the 1980s encouraged the finance, insurance, and real estate sectors—collectively, the FIRE sector—to interweave so tightly as to be deemed a single sector. As this sector devised new ways to increase its income and assets, the economy's center of gravity shifted. Less of GDP went to manufacturing, more to finance. Less to regular people, more to the financial elite.[21]

In the postwar years, manufacturing—making things in the real economy—was close to 30 percent of US GDP, while financial services was 11 percent. By 2000, this had flipped. FIRE sector revenues reached 20 percent of GDP; manufacturing slipped below 15 percent. As Phillips put it, the economy shifted from manufacturing stuff to manufacturing debt.[22]

We can visualize the danger of this if we picture the financial economy as a sphere dwelling above the real economy, tapping its energy—like a debt load sitting on your shoulders. The financial economy is essentially a collection of assets, like stocks, bonds, loans, and mortgages. These are all claims against the real economy. Every dollar one person owes as debt is held by someone else as an asset. Equity in companies works similarly; stockholders have a claim against company earnings.

Consider the UK, for example. In 1990, private sector financial assets (securities, loans, equities, pensions, insurance) were about four times GDP. The debt load was four times as big as the economy that supported it. But as financial extraction revved into high gear—more mortgages, more profits, more debt—the sum of financial claims ballooned. By the year 2006, this debt load had swollen to *double* its previous size in relation to GDP. Now the sphere of debt was *eight* times as big as the economy supporting it. Similar trends were happening in the US and elsewhere.[23]

This set the stage for the 2008 collapse. As mortgage lenders ran out of reasonable mortgages to write, they began to issue reckless ones that could never be paid back. The house of financial wealth was becoming too large. Yet because the system's essence was insatiability, its logic could not comprehend the idea of too much financial wealth. Thus more claims—and more absurd claims—were manufactured until the debt load exceeded the load-bearing capacity of the real economy. The system entered a phase of financial overshoot, much like ecological overshoot.[24]

Governments responded by propping up the overbuilt system. That prepared the way for the cycle to repeat itself. As UK economic analyst Howard Reed observed, the financial sector in the UK shrank after the financial crash, but began expanding again in 2015. "More shockingly," he wrote, "total UK private sector debt—including securities, loans, equities and insurance—rose from 430 percent of GDP in 1990 to 960 percent in 2017."[25] (See Figure 2. Definition of debt is securities, loans, equities, pensions, and insurance in the private sector—corporate and household, not government debt.)

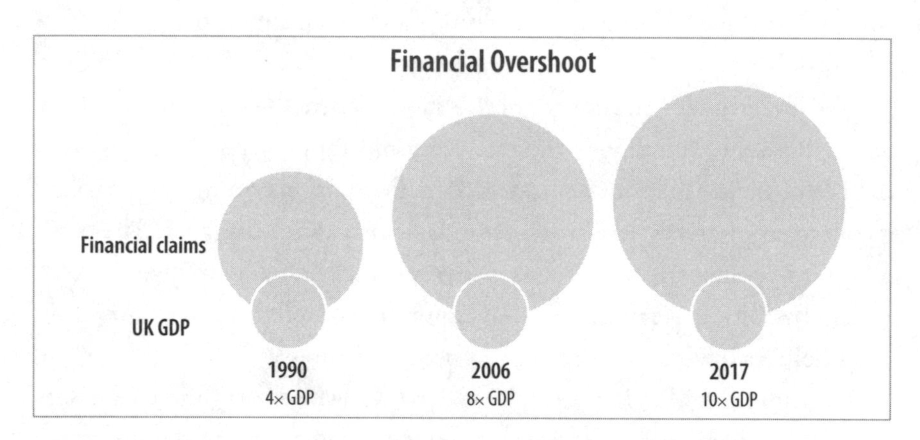

FIGURE 2. The UK private sector debt load in relation to GDP doubled between 1990 and 2006, from four to eight times GDP, helping trigger the 2008 crisis. Yet today, the UK private sector debt load is larger, 10 times GDP.[26]

In short: Private sector financial claims in the UK are now nearly *ten times* GDP. No living system grows rapidly forever. Cancer attempts to do so, and in the process, kills its host.

The notion that finance is sucking too much out of the real economy is not an abstraction in places like Preston and elsewhere in the north of England. Wealth is systematically extracted from them and then controlled by the City of London, the British analog of Wall Street. On a per capita basis, the government also invests half as much in the North as it does in London, according to John McDonnell of the Labour Party.[27]

The problem with extractive economy finance is not only that it is unfair to working people, drives perpetual growth, and contributes to ecological crises, it's that the system is programmed for its own implosion. It is a snake devouring its tail.

The IMF has warned of "storm clouds" gathering for a new financial crisis; billionaire investor Paul Tudor Jones has highlighted a "global debt bubble"; and fund manager Jim Rogers has predicted a financial crash that will be the biggest in his 76 years. The financial community has taken to talk of the "everything bubble"—the massive runup in the value of stocks, real estate, and other assets—with the *New York Times* asking, "what might prove the pinprick"?[28]

PATHWAYS FOR ETHICAL FINANCE

For those interested in building the democratic economy, the question is: Will government again prop up the extractive system? Or can we seize the opportunity to advance democratic economy finance? There is "another way forward, grounded in long-term public ownership of financial institutions," writes our colleague Thomas Hanna. In the last crisis, the US government de facto nationalized some of the big financial players, only to later simply return them to private ownership. In the UK, the government still holds control of the big bank RBS, which taxpayers bailed out in 2008 to the tune of £45 billion. The New Economics Foundation has proposed bringing RBS wholly into public ownership, breaking it into a network of 130 local banks. In the US, Hanna has similarly proposed that in the next crisis, policymakers consider converting failed banks to permanent public ownership.[29] It would be wise for progressives to have such a plan in place. What seems outlandish one day can become eminently practical in a crisis.

There are many other pathways for ethical finance to advance—including through responsible investment processes such as fossil fuel divestment, support for green bonds, and impact investing. The largest generational transfer of wealth in history—$50 trillion—is coming, with the passing of the Baby Boom generation.[30] Many inheritors will be women, who are known to be disposed toward ethical investing, as are many millennial investors.[31]

Imagine if we invested not only for people and planet, but to advance democratic economy institutions that create broad-based asset ownership—ensuring great wealth never again accumulates in the hands of a tiny elite. One such approach is investing in employee ownership. Back in Cleveland, the new Fund for Employee Ownership was recently launched by the leaders of the Evergreen Cooperatives, Brett Jones and John McMicken, working with our colleague Jessica Rose as strategic adviser. It's housed at the Evergreen Cooperative Development Fund, which helped finance the Evergreen Cooperative Laundry—the place Chris Brown landed after three years in prison, and where he advanced to plant supervisor.

The fund will purchase privately held companies and convert them to employee ownership, creating good work, anchoring wealth in community, and generating value for investors. After proof of concept in Northeast Ohio, the fund plans to go national. The aim is to demonstrate how mission-driven capital can be leveraged to help business owners sell their firms, offering them "an experience that's as frictionless as any other exit option they have available to them," Jessica said.[32]

At The Democracy Collaborative, we believe capital is the missing partner needed to take employee ownership to scale. Investment banker Dick May of American Working Capital suggests that $100 billion in federal loan guarantees would create a magnet for private capital that would support the creation of 13 million new employee owners in a decade, doubling today's number.[33] That's just one example of the vital role capital can play in building a democratic economy.

✦ ✦ ✦

As more cities began to call on Matthew Brown, Ted found funding to enable him to become a senior fellow at The Democracy Collaborative, enabling him to devote full time to spreading the Preston Model. "I'm finally free," Matthew told us. For Matthew, free means working 50 to 60 hours a week and traveling nonstop.

"Eight to nine London Councils are interested," he said. "The Scottish government shows interest. The Welsh assembly is looking at it. Also the Metro Mayor of Liverpool," he added. "You're talking a hell of a lot. We were even invited to speak with the Number 10 policy unit in Downing St. There's something in that."[34]

In the early days, "when I was coming up with all these ideas, people liked them, but they said, can this work?" he recalled. Now, "people are excited." For 40 years, there's been no alternative, "just managed decline." But now, "With the pension fund, anchor procurement, the living wage, worker co-ops getting started, the credit union, the bank," Matthew said, "we're really building a democratic economy."

CONCLUSION
FROM AN EXTRACTIVE TO A DEMOCRATIC ECONOMY

Thoughts on next steps for the pathway ahead

> Most of the things worth doing in the world had been declared impossible before they were done.
>
> —LOUIS BRANDEIS

"We're in a systemic crisis, and no one is dealing head-on with it," Gar said to the board of trustees of The Democracy Collaborative who were seated around the conference table in our Washington, DC, office. The meeting was our first after the 2018 US mid-term elections, and the board was discussing what the shift in control of the US House of Representatives could mean. "This is not just about more policies," Gar reminded us. "I don't think this is a question of how you assemble allies. How do we clarify what a moral system is which includes everybody?"

"We need policies," Gar continued. But the crisis is at the level of the system, the deep tectonic level of institutional designs that keep the status quo functioning, the unquestioned assumptions that

make troubling outcomes seem normal. "Our work," he said, "is to help people see, here are the things that we can build now, in the real world, that point toward a different system."

What Gar was talking about came up in a slightly different form when the two of us, Marjorie and Ted, spoke to a group of fellow travelers doing economic change work. An audience member asked, "What's the benefit if we see ourselves as a unified group?" Implicit was a sense that, well, we'll all still get up tomorrow and advance our separate battles. How can it matter if we see ourselves as all working for a next system?

In her famous essay on "Leverage Points: Places to Intervene in a System," systems theorist Donella Meadows observed that there are many ways to shift system behavior—creating taxes, regulating bad behavior, adding incentives, bringing lawsuits, designing new structures, shifting who holds power. Yet the most effective place to intervene, she wrote, is at the level of *mindset*. The "great big unstated assumptions," she wrote, "constitute that society's paradigm, or deepest set of beliefs about how the world works." The paradigm is the source of the system.[1]

The system arises from our "shared social agreements about the nature of reality," Meadows said.[2] We all know today's economic reality: Investors are owners and employees are hired hands. The corporation is an object that can be owned and sold. Financial wealth is the scarcest commodity and therefore the most precious. Its growth is ideally limitless. Fiduciary duty to investors is the most important moral duty in the investing and corporate world. GDP and balance sheets count everything that counts. Income to labor is an expense to be reduced. There's no such thing as too much profit or too much wealth. People are poor because it's their own fault.

A different paradigm doesn't start with capital as the center of the universe. It starts from the point of view of life. And reality looks something like this: there's only one system, the earth, which is precious beyond measure. The economy and everything in it are subsets of this one system. There are limits to growth. Companies are human communities, living systems, and workers are naturally members. Wise stewardship of our common assets, our common well-being, is the aim of the economy, its institutions, and activities. We're in this together and all have a right to human dignity. Everyone deserves the opportunity to thrive, with extra assistance owed to those long excluded, on whose backs the old system was built.

When we see with moral clarity, it becomes blindingly obvious that a democracy is about the pursuit of happiness for everyone. Democracy in the polity and democracy in the economy are the left and right hands of the good society.

THE MORAL FORCE OF LEGITIMACY

Seeing this is much like seeing that people of color are human beings equal in dignity to whites, that women are human beings not subordinate to men, or that there's no such thing as the divine right of kings. These are world-changing insights. They're simple truths that are self-evident. When we see such truths, old institutions built on archaic assumptions begin to crumble. They lose legitimacy. And without legitimacy, no system long endures, regardless of how much power it seems to possess.

Apartheid fell in South Africa. The monarchy is a shadow of its former self. The #MeToo movement has brought down countless men of power. When we the people withdraw legitimacy, we undermine the ground of cultural acceptance that biased behavior relies upon. We exercise not brute force but moral force.

Moral power comes from moral unity. Women became a unified force in recognizing sex bias. Economic actors will become a unified force when we recognize capital bias. Common seeing creates power. As linguist George Lakoff has put it, effective naming isn't about clever wordsmithing; it's about seeing reality clearly.[3]

If legitimacy is one potent tool we possess, a second tool is imagination. This is the work of imaginative excellence so critical at a time when old institutions, old ways, are creating crises. We see this in the imaginative development of concepts like the anchor mission, impact investing, social justice in economic development, community wealth building, employee ownership, B Corporations, social determinants of health, public banking, and more. This is the pattern language of a democratic economy in formation. The more of us who use these terms and approaches, the more powerful they become. We're stronger together. In an appendix, we offer a starting list of organizations to consider partnering with.

VOICES FOR DEEP CHANGE

In all of this, expressing moral intent can be as important as action. When the Rockefeller Brothers Fund and the Rockefeller Family Fund—heirs to the original oil fortune of John D. Rockefeller—announced plans to divest from fossil fuel companies, they gave both moral and financial reasons for doing so.[4] In the process, they helped others shift the underlying erroneous assumption that morality has no role in investing.

Divesting from fossil fuels and shifting to impact investing are steps many of us can take. Some $8 trillion has already been divested, including by the pension funds of the Republic of Ireland, London, and New York City, as well as churches and universities.[5] As individuals, we can study the index funds we're in for fossil fuel holdings. We can find funds and advisers focused on impact investing. Young MBAs and finance professionals can build the new vehicles needed to make impact investing more accessible.

With banking relationships, we can shift our money to locally owned banks, credit unions, and cooperative banks—and ask our institutions (churches, pension funds, local government) to do the same. Move Your Money is a group that can help.[6]

Charitable donations deserve the same scrutiny. We need to continue supporting food banks and other ways people excluded from the system survive. But we might carve out 5 to 10 percent or more for system-changing kinds of organizations.

Bolder philanthropic moves can be catalytic. Edgar Villanueva, in his book *Decolonizing Wealth*, suggests that philanthropy could enact a racial reparations project—with each foundation tithing 10 percent of assets to a trust fund, to which Native Americans and African Americans could apply for grants for asset-building projects.[7]

All this is what's possible when we think seriously about how we invest and donate our money. And then imagine what happens when we all bring the same moral intent to how we design and build our businesses, how and from whom we purchase, how we let real estate be developed, how we ask our cities to support businesses, and so on. Armed with the knowledge that there are realistic alternatives, we can begin to make the kind of bold choices that put us on a path toward a more democratic economy.

AREAS OFF LIMITS TO EXTRACTION

In intellectual terms, large questions remain to be tackled, like what to do with major corporations. What's needed is a concerted corporate redesign effort—perhaps including a government commission, a think tank project doing research and convening, and an academic network pursuing research. We at The Democracy Collaborative call this "next generation enterprise design," and we've begun it via exploratory research and convening around employee-owned benefit corporations.[8]

We also need large rethinking about the economy overall—for example, which kinds of ownership and control are most appropriate for various sectors? We need bold ideas for limiting the reach of extraction—putting some areas of the economy off limits to profit maximization. An example is single-payer healthcare, which implicitly says healthcare is a human right too important to be left to control by extractive companies.

Publicly owned pharmaceutical companies are a related concept. A transformed, democratically controlled pharmaceutical industry working for the public good would be a powerful example (and important pillar) of a democratic economy focused on well-being, not profits.[9] Even one major new model like public pharma could begin to shift the mindset that profit-maximizing corporations should control everything.

Another large issue is the growth of technology and the new world coming where far less work will be needed. Who should own the robots? Since technology is mainly socially created knowledge, its fruits should be distributed socially to one and all, Gar says.[10] How could that be done?

If long-term thinking is needed, we also need ideas that are actionable soon, with a movement to make them a reality. As Gar told the trustees that day, "There will be a moment when Trump is gone. How do we position ourselves to be ready?" System-changing issues are on the policy agenda today more than at any time in memory—and whether or not these pass immediately, they start conversations that need starting.

There are many other points of intervention. Echoing scientist Thomas Kuhn, the creator of the concept of paradigms, Donella Meadows talked about many ways to change a paradigm: pointing to the anomalies and failures in the old paradigm, bringing people with the new paradigm into positions of visibility and power, and modeling the next system.

RADICAL HOPE

What we're doing is escaping from the grip of the long arm of finance and extraction—first of all in our minds. We can start in our own communities. In building community wealth, the locus is not an amorphous, global economy, but regular people in one geographic place. The aim is ownership locally rooted there, and broadly held. Instead of decision making by an absentee elite, power is brought back within the circle of community. Money recirculates, multiplying and enriching as it flows. People and organizations work collaboratively, not in isolation. The focus is on assets, not problems—on empowerment, not dependency. There's sensitivity to place—what works in Preston may not be the same as in Cleveland—and to culture: the language that resonates with white Rust Belt factory workers will be different from what inspires Lakota young people on Pine Ridge. And different from what inspires a room of hospital purchasing directors, or a gathering of impact investors—even though the core message remains the same. Woven throughout is deliberate inclusion for those long excluded, the marginalized, now at the center. The seed of it is radical hope, formed in desperate circumstances. And even as we read or talk about all of this, or witness it in microcosm, it begins to take shape in the mind: a democratic economy, recognizably and coherently in formation.

It begins simply with seeing. "You could say paradigms are harder to change than anything else about a system," Donella Meadows wrote. "But there's nothing physical or expensive or even slow about paradigm change. In a single individual it can happen in a millisecond. All it takes is a click in the mind, a new way of seeing."[11]

AFTERWORD

It seemed such a small, foolhardily ignorable venture. There was the news bursting with the hugest stories in decades—Trump, Brexit, the revival of fascism across Europe—and here was I, a journalist for *The Guardian*, focusing on some of the tiniest. My year, I'd decided, would be dedicated to meeting and writing about communities far from the centers of power. The ones who'd seen their factories shut 30 years ago and then, in the past decade, watched their friends and families devastated by historic spending cuts. These were often places too far from London to catch the attention of Westminster and the media, and too obscure for most Britons to care about. Preston, an hour away from Manchester. Plymouth, at the end of the trainline. The light-industrial estates of East Kilbride in Scotland. You get the picture. In journalistic terms, I might as well have picked up a lance and checked Google Maps for the nearest windmill.

But what drew me to these places wasn't the chance to tell more sad stories. It was because these communities had realized that solutions to their ills weren't to be found from a visiting government minister or in the contract with a multinational. No, if these people wanted to fix things, they'd have to do it themselves. Like Theresa MacDermott and Eleanor Lee in Liverpool, who first stopped their houses getting knocked down and then turned themselves into community property developers, building affordable homes to be rented out to locals. Or council member Chris Penberthy in Plymouth, on a shoestring budget, working to launch a postindustrial network of social enterprises that employs over 7,000 local residents. Or John Clark and Alistair Miller, who wanted to retire from their printing business outside Glasgow but didn't want some pinstriped vultures picking over the balance sheet, so they took the risk of selling it to their 60 employees.

I knew I found these people and their politics compelling, but what caught me off-guard was the vociferousness of readers' response. These pieces were shared on social media over and over, letters and emails poured in; a podcast that we started is still attracting correspondence. Local and national politicians and activists got in touch to find out more. One story I wrote, about a speck of a town in the middle of Germany that faced down a giant energy company to take back their electric grid, got fervent letters from the Faroe Islands to find out how they could do the same. The series was extended, by reader demand, for many more installments than I had originally anticipated. We held a live discussion in Preston, which even without marketing sold out once, and when we moved it to a much larger venue it sold out again. And once the evening was over, some of the audience ended up in the grocery store opposite where, I'm told, they continued the discussion in the middle of the fruit and vegetable aisle.

Why the popularity? Partly because these were great stories, as I hope you can tell. But more than that, they disproved the orthodoxy distilled four decades ago by Margaret Thatcher into one pungent phrase: There Is No Alternative. There is no alternative, that is, apart from handing money to the rich, hacking at the public realm, giving more power to financial centers and relying on finance to be your golden goose. Well, 10 years after the banking crash destroyed Thatcher's world, here were the alternatives—and readers wanted to know more.

These alternatives aren't perfect, by any means. These are real people working within real constraints, often on little money and a lot of caffeine. But they are working to invent a future worth living in for themselves, their families and their communities. In the book you have just read, Marjorie Kelly and Ted Howard tell the same kind of stories.

Like Kelly and Howard, when I set out to explore how our economy might be reacquainted with the concept of democracy, I looked for the experiments rather than templates. In time, I hope to see these alternatives grow. That doesn't mean replicating identical copies of what worked in Preston or Cleveland. A democratic economy should be one with a lot of diversity, reflecting the needs and desires of people who live there. But to make it happen, we need to take on what Kelly and Howard call *capital bias*—the structures that keep alternatives starved for the resources they need to keep the lights on, while a firehose of financialized money continues fueling the parts of our economy that are creating the problems in the first place, raising rents, extracting wealth, and spewing ever more carbon into the air.

Most of our lives do not run at the ultra-fast tempo that the political and media worlds dictate. Our lives aren't fast-moving stories and late-breaking news. Surveys in the UK of what people actually want out of an economy are surprisingly rare, but one was published by the hard-right Legatum think tank in 2017. Top priorities for respondents were, in order: food and water; emergency services; universal healthcare; a good house; a decent well-paying job; and compulsory and free education. At the bottom were owning a car, social media, and cheap air travel.

Reading the Legatum's gloss of the survey, you can almost feel the level of confusion. At the end, its authors concluded: "Significant portions of the country ... are vehemently anti-capitalist." When the dominant worldview of our times treats the public's desire for basics such as food and water as ideologically suspect, you know it's a time for an Alternative.

—ADITYA CHAKRABORTTY, senior economics commentator and columnist for *The Guardian*

APPENDIX
NETWORKS OF THE DEMOCRATIC ECONOMY

To help readers get involved, we offer here a list—by no means comprehensive or exhaustive—of organizations working on elements of the democratic economy. Many of the national and international groups listed here have local partners or affiliates doing the ground work in specific communities.

INEQUALITY, RACIAL EQUITY, AND CAPITAL BIAS

Action Center on Race and the Economy (ACRE) Institute: Campaign hub connecting struggles for racial justice with engaged research into the extractive, financialized economy.

https://www.acreinstitute.org

Institute for Policy Studies: Movement-oriented progressive think tank dedicated to building a more equitable, ecologically sustainable, and peaceful society.

https://ips-dc.org

PolicyLink: Research and advocacy organization dedicated to the idea that "equity is the superior growth model."

https://www.policylink.org

Roosevelt Institute: Policy and research think tank advancing ways to rewrite the rules of our unequal economy.

http://rooseveltinstitute.org

ORGANIZING AND ADVOCACY FOR A DEMOCRATIC ECONOMY

Community Change: Building the power and capacity of low-income people, especially low-income people of color, to fight for their communities' future.

https://communitychange.org

Cooperation Jackson (Mississippi): Inspiring local effort to advance an economy based in solidarity and self-determination in the deep South.

https://cooperationjackson.org

Democratic Socialists of America: Rapidly growing membership organization making a once-taboo word a force in practical local organizing.

https://www.dsausa.org

NDN Collective: Platform for building indigenous power to advance transformative solutions.

https://ndncollective.org

New Economy Coalition: Brings together 200+ organizations into a network and platform for advancing a new economy.

https://neweconomy.net

New Economy Project (NYC): Organizing campaigns against the abuses of the current economy and for transformative solutions.

https://www.neweconomynyc.org

People's Action: National network building community power to advance long-term change.

https://peoplesaction.org

FINANCE AND INVESTING

Global Impact Investing Network (GIIN): International knowledge exchange to accelerate impact investment.

https://thegiin.org

National Community Reinvestment Coalition: Association of 600+ community-based organizations fighting against disinvestment and discrimination in the financial system.

https://ncrc.org

Public Banking Institute: Hub of research and advocacy into publicly owned financial alternatives.

https://www.publicbankinginstitute.org

Social Capital Markets (SOCAP): Network and platform to advance impact investment and social entrepreneurship.

https://socialcapitalmarkets.net

The Working World: Innovative nonprofit lender fueling the development of worker cooperatives with non-extractive finance.

https://www.theworkingworld.org

EMPLOYEE OWNERSHIP AND PROGRESSIVE BUSINESS

American Sustainable Business Council: Roundtable representing 250,000 businesses committed to a triple bottom line.

http://asbcouncil.org

B Lab: A nonprofit organization that serves a global movement of people using business as a force for good.

https://bcorporation.net/

Democracy at Work Institute: Research institute developing resources for the worker cooperative sector.

https://institute.coop

The ESOP Association: National lobbying organization for Employee Stock Ownership Plans, with regional chapters for companies.

https://www.esopassociation.org/

ICA Group: Longstanding center developing innovative models for democratic workplaces.

https://ica-group.org

National Center for Employee Ownership: Clearinghouse for information and research on employee ownership.

https://www.nceo.org

Project Equity: Advancing employee ownership solutions for business owners, local policymakers, and community advocates.

https://www.project-equity.org

EQUITABLE LOCAL ECONOMIES

BALLE (Business Alliance for Local Living Economies): Convener and network builder advancing equity and sustainability in finance and business development.

https://bealocalist.org

Hope Nation: Consulting firm advancing community wealth building in Native communities.

https://www.hopenationconsulting.com

REDF (Roberts Enterprise Development Fund): Social enterprise accelerator that has helped create over 30,000 jobs for people facing barriers to employment.

https://redf.org

LAND, HOUSING, AND COMMUNITY CONTROL

Center for Community Progress: Develops strategies to reclaim urban space for community-led development.

https://www.communityprogress.net

Grounded Solutions Network: Network of research and practice advancing permanently affordable, community-controlled housing.

https://groundedsolutions.org

Right to the City Alliance: Social movement network advancing housing and urban justice.

https://righttothecity.org

HEALTHY COMMUNITIES

Build Healthy Places Network: Platform exploring the intersections of health equity and community development.

https://www.buildhealthyplaces.org

Health Care Without Harm: Catalyzing leadership on sustainability in the healthcare sector.

https://noharm.org

The Root Cause Coalition: Cross-sector collaboration tackling the social determinants of community health.

https://www.rootcausecoalition.org

JUST TRANSITION

Asian Pacific Environmental Network (Oakland): Base-building and organizing for environmental justice.

https://apen4ej.org

Climate Justice Alliance: Grassroots network of frontline communities fighting for an equitable response to climate crisis.

https://climatejusticealliance.org

Emerald Cities Collaborative: Creating high road economic development strategies for local sustainability.

http://emeraldcities.org

Oil Change International: Research and advocacy around the urgent need to shut down fossil fuel extraction.

http://priceofoil.org

Sunrise Movement: Youth-driven activism agitating for a Green New Deal.

https://www.sunrisemovement.org

Uprose (NYC): Community-based mobilization to connect urban justice to climate adaptation and resilience.

https://www.uprose.org

OUTSIDE THE US

CLES (Centre for Local Economic Strategies) (UK): Advancing a vision of economies grounded in community wealth building.

https://cles.org.uk

Momentum (UK): Grassroots network building power for transformative change.

https://peoplesmomentum.com

New Economics Foundation (UK): Research institute advancing policy solutions for economic justice.

https://neweconomics.org

New Economy Organisers Network (UK): Developing strategic interventions to build movement capacity and shift the conversation around politics and the economy.

https://neweconomyorganisers.org

Transnational Institute (Amsterdam): Multisector think tank advancing a vision of an economy serving the public good.

https://www.tni.org

NOTES

INTRODUCTION

1 Dale Maharidge, "A Photographic Chronicle of America's Working Poor," *Smithsonian Magazine*, December 2016.

2 "From John Adams to Mercy Otis Warren, 16 April 1776," *Founders Online*, National Archives, January 18, 2019, *https://founders.archives.gov/documents/Adams/06-04-02-0044*.

3 Aldo Leopold, *A Sand County Almanac* (New York: Oxford University Press, 1966), 217–18.

4 Gordon S. Wood, *The Radicalism of the American Revolution* (New York: Random House, 1991), 8.

5 Michelle Alexander, "We Are Not the Resistance," *New York Times*, September 23, 2018.

6 "From John Adams to Thomas Jefferson, 19 December 1813," *Founders Online*, National Archives, January 18, 2019, *https://founders.archives.gov/documents/Adams/99-02-02-6212*.

7 Larry Elliott, "World's 26 Richest People Own as Much as Poorest 50%, Says Oxfam," *The Guardian*, January 20, 2019.

8 Chuck Collins and Josh Hoxie, *Billionaire Bonanza: The Forbes 400 and the Rest of Us*, (Washington, DC: Institute for Policy Studies, November 2017), 2.

9 Data from Berkeley economics professor Immanuel Saez, cited by Josh Baro, "95% of Income Gains Since 2009 Went to the Top 1%—Here's What That Really Means," *Business Insider*, September 12, 2013, *https://www.businessinsider.com/95-of-income-gains-since-2009-went-to-the-top-1-heres-what-that-really-means-2013-9*.

10 Federal Reserve, "Executive Summary" from *Report on the Economic Well Being of U.S. Households in 2017* (Washington, DC: Board of Governors of the Federal Reserve System, May 2018), 2.

11 Humanity is currently using nature 1.7 times faster than our planet's ecosystems can regenerate. World Wildlife Fund, *Living Planet Report—2018: Aiming Higher*, M. Grooten and R. E. A. Almond, Eds., (Glands, Switzerland: World Wildlife Fund, 2018).

12 Mathew Lawrence, Laurie Laybourn-Langton, and Carys Roberts, "The Road to Ruin: Making Sense of the Anthropocene," *Institute for Progressive Policy Research* 24, no. 3 (2017).

13 World Wildlife Fund, *Living Planet Report—Risk and Resilience in a New Era* (Glands, Switzerland: WWF International, 2016).

14 Joseph Stiglitz, "Of the 1%, By the 1%, For the 1%," *Vanity Fair*, May 2011.

15 GAO, *Contingent Workforce: Size, Characteristics, Earnings, and Benefits* (Washington, DC: US Government Accountability Office, April 20, 2015), *https://www.gao.gov/assets/670/669766.pdf*.

16 Eillie Anzilotti, "Elizabeth Warren's Bold New Plan to Give Corporate Wealth Back to Workers," *Fast Company*, August 22, 2018.

17 Peter Gowan, remarks at Rutgers University (Mid-Year Fellows Workshop on employee ownership, New Brunswick, NJ, January 13, 2019).

18 Jimmy Tobias, "What If People Owned the Banks, Instead of Wall Street?" *The Nation*, May 22, 2017.

19 Jonathan Lear, *Radical Hope: Ethics in the Face of Cultural Devastation* (Cambridge, MA: Harvard University Press, 2006), 7, 94–5, 103, 113, 117–18.

20 Donella Meadows, *Thinking in Systems: A Primer* (White River Junction, VT: Chelsea Green Publishing, 2008). Quote is from Donella Meadows, "Places to Intervene in a System," *Whole Earth*, Winter 1997.

21 Elena Kadvany, "Feeding Families," *Palo Alto Weekly*, July 24, 2015.

22 *New State Ice Co. v. Liebmann*, 285 US 262(1932).

23 Heather Long, "71% of Americans Believe Economy Is 'rigged,'" *CNN Business*, June 28, 2016, *http://money.cnn.com/2016/06/28/news/economy/americans-believe-economy-is-rigged/index.html*.

24 George Eaton, "How Preston—the UK's 'Most Improved City'—Became a Success Story for Corbynomics," *New Statesman*, November 1, 2018.

25 Steve Dubb, "Historic Federal Law Gives Employee-Owned Businesses Access to SBA Loans," *Nonprofit Quarterly*, August 14, 2018.

26 Rochdale Stronger Together, accessed February 26, 2019, *http://rochdalestrongertogether.org.uk/*.

27 Michael Haederle, "Healthy Neighborhoods Albuquerque Aims to Create Main Street Jobs," *University of New Mexico Health Sciences Newsroom*, September 27, 2016, *http://hsc-news.unm.edu/news/healthy-neighborhoods-albuquerque-ams-to-create-main-street-jobs*.

28 Chris Brown, email to Sarah Stranahan, December 10, 2018.

29 James E. Causey, "In Cleveland, Co-op Model Finds Hope in Employers Rooted in the City," *Milwaukee Journal Sentinel*, April 27, 2017. Other details from John McMicken, interview with Ted Howard, January 3, 2019, and email from John McMicken, January 5, 2019.

30 Maharidge, "Photographic Chronicle of Working Poor."

CHAPTER 1

1 See *https://bealocalist.org/first-immersion-balle-rsf-community-foundation-circle*. Also see "Aligning Money with Mission," Local Economy Foundation Circle, *https://bealocalist.org/local-foundation-circle/*.

2 Tech Dump, *https://www.techdump.org/who-we-are/*; Impact Recyclers, *https://impactrecyclers.com/our-members/*; Social Enterprise Alliance, *https://socialenterprise.us/*.

3 "Rush System for Health: Annual Report for the Fiscal Year Ended June 30, 2018, Audited," *https://www.rush.edu/sites/default/files/fy2018-annual-report-0618.pdf*.

4 Rush University Medical Center, "The Anchor Mission Playbook," The Democracy Collaborative, September 19, 2017, *https://democracycollaborative.org/content/anchor-mission-playbook*.

5 Marjorie Kelly and Sarah McKinley, *Cities Building Community Wealth* (Washington, DC: The Democracy Collaborative, November 2015), *https://democracycollaborative.org/cities*.

6 Michelle Stearn, "Green Taxi Cooperative: Building an Alternative to the Corporate 'Sharing Economy,'" The Democracy Collaborative, May 19, 2016, *https://democracycollaborative.org/content/green-taxi-cooperative-building-alternative-corporate-sharing-economy*.

7 NCEO, "New Data on Number of ESPOs and Participants," *Employee Ownership Report*, March–April 2019.

8 Sarah Stranahan, "Eileen Fisher: Designing for Change," Fifty by Fifty, August 15, 2018, *https://medium.com/fifty-by-fifty/eileen-fisher-designing-for-change-f6877b4130f1*; Sarah Stranahan, "Employee-Owned B Corp Makes a Great Brew," Fifty by Fifty, December 5, 2018, *https://medium.com/fifty-by-fifty/employee-owned-b-corp-makes-a-great-brew-6cb21df7b56d*.

9 John Lewis Partnership, "Now and the Future," John Lewis Partnership, PLC, Annual Report and Accounts 2018, *https://www.johnlewispartnership.co.uk/content/dam/cws/pdfs/financials/annual-reports/jlp-annual-report-and-accounts-2018.pdf*.

10 Unofficial estimate by B Lab as of June 19, 2018; *https://bcorporation.net/about-b-lab*.

11 Mondragon worker count and revenue from "About Mondragon," Mondragon S Coop, accessed January 5, 2019, *https://www.mondragon-corporation.com/en/about-us/economic-and-financial-indicators/corporate-profile/*.

12 Michael Toye, "Participate Now in the Social Innovation and Social Finance Strategy Consultations," Canadian CED Network, November 23, 2017, *https://ccednet-rcdec.ca/en/blog/2017/11/23/participate-now-social-innovation-and-social-finance.* "Quebec Budget: $100 Million for the Social Economy Despite Some Disappointments," Canadian CED Network, April 6, 2015, *https://ccednet-rcdec.ca/en/new-in-ced/2015/04/06/quebec-budget-100-million-social-economy-despite-some.*

13 "Remunicipalization," Municipal Services Project: Exploring Alternatives to Privatization, accessed February 11, 2019, *https://www.municipalservicesproject.org/remunicipalization.*

14 Thomas M. Hanna, *Our Common Wealth: The Return of Public Ownership in the United States* (Manchester, England: Manchester University Press, 2018), 3, 9.

15 Hanna, Our Common Wealth, 11.

16 The CDFI Fund website lists 1,112 certified CDFIs as of September 30, 2018; United States Department of the Treasury, "Investing for the Future," Community Development Financial Institutions Fund, *https://www.cdfifund.gov/Pages/default.aspx.*

17 Amit Bouri, "Impact Investing: The Next Big Movement," *Medium*, May 9, 2018, *https://medium.com/@AmitKBouri/impact-investing-the-next-big-movement-b782de8a32d5.*

18 Stanford Encyclopedia of Philosophy, "Dewey's Political Philosophy," Stanford Center for the Study of Language and Information, July 26, 2018, *https://plato.stanford.edu/entries/dewey-political/.*

19 Amartya Sen, *Development as Freedom* (New York: Knopf, 1999).

20 This definition of capital bias—which is original to *The Making of a Democratic Economy*—draws on the definition of racial bias given by Robin J. DiAngelo, "Whiteness in Racial Dialogue: A Discourse Analysis" (PhS diss. University of Washington, 2004), 2, *https://digital.lib.washington.edu/researchworks/handle/1773/7867.*

21 Herman E. Daly and John B. Cobb, Jr., *For the Common Good* (Boston: Beacon Press, 1989), 5–8, 86–7.

22 BEA, "Gross Domestic Product by Industry: Second Quarter 2018," Bureau of Economic Analysis, November 1, 2018, 10–11, *https://www.bea.gov/system/files/2018-10/gdpind218_1.pdf.*

23 Kelly and McKinley, *Cities Building Community Wealth*, 21.

24 Ted DeHaven, "Corporate Welfare in the Federal Budget," Cato Institute, Policy Analysis, July 25, 2012.

25 Edward N. Wolff, "Household Wealth Trends in the United States, 1962–2016," National Bureau of Economic Research Working Paper No. 24085, November 2017.

26 Martha Nussbaum, *Creating Capabilities: The Human Development Approach* (Cambridge, MA: Harvard University Press, 2011).

27 Abraham Lincoln, "Annual Message to Congress," December 3, 1861, House Divided: The Civil War Research Engine at Dickinson College, *http://hd.housedivided.dickinson.edu/node/40507.*

28 Marjorie Kelly, "The Divine Right of Capital," Fifty by Fifty, January 17, 2018, *https://medium.com/fifty-by-fifty/the-divine-right-of-capital-d6e8cd57f8c7*.

29 Carina Millstone, *Frugal Value: Designing Business for a Crowded Planet* (New York: Routledge, 2017).

30 Marjorie Kelly, *The Divine Right of Capital* (San Francisco: Berrett-Koehler Publishers, 2001).

31 "Report of the World Commission on Environment and Development: Our Common Future," UN, 1987, *http://www.un-documents.net/our-common-future.pdf*.

32 George Lakoff, interview with Marjorie Kelly, August 24, 2006.

CHAPTER 2

1 Visit to Pine Ridge, May 28–29, 2015. For information on the Learning/Action Lab of The Democracy Collaborative, see *https://lab.community-wealth.org/*.

2 Quoted in Joyce Appleby, *Capitalism and a New Social Order* (New York: New York University Press, 1984), 95.

3 Richard White, "Born Modern: An Overview of the West," *History Now: Journal of the Gilder Lehrman Institute*, Fall 2006, *http://ap.gilderlehrman.org/essays/born-modern-overview-west?period=6*.

4 John G. Neihardt, *Black Elk Speaks* (New York: William Morrow and Company, 1932), 7–8.

5 Jay Walljasper, "Healthy Snack Invented on Indian Reservation Now Faces Stiff Corporate Competition," *Common Dreams*, August 10, 2016.

6 Cynthia E. Smith, Curator of Socially Responsible Design, "By the People: Designing a Better America," on display September 30, 2016–February 26, 2017 at the Cooper Hewitt Smithsonian Design Museum in Manhattan.

7 Sarah Sunshine Manning, "A Community Self-Empowerment Model for Indian Country: Thunder Valley CDC, Part I," *Indian Country Today*, January 15, 2016.

8 Manning, "Community Self-Empowerment Model."

9 "Sustainable Housing Ownership Project," Thunder Valley Community Development Corporation, accessed on February 11, 2019, *https://thundervalley.org/program-guide/sustainable-home-ownership-project*.

10 Nick Tilsen on many occasions has publicly told the story of the message received from the elders. This quote is taken from remarks by Nick in a video entitled, "Ecosystem of Opportunity: Thunder Valley CDC Documentary," produced by Thunder Valley CDC, aired May 8, 2015, on YouTube, *https://www.youtube.com/watch?v=-6aBQ09SjNI*.

11 Annie Lowrey, "Pain on the Reservation," *New York Times*, July 12, 2013, *https://www.nytimes.com/2013/07/13/business/economy/us-budget-cuts-fall-heavily-on-american-indians.html*.

12 Megan Huynh,"Creating an ecosystem of opportunity on Pine Ridge," The Democracy Collaborative, June 6, 2018, *https://community-wealth.org/content/creating-ecosystem-opportunity-pine-ridge.*

13 These comments are drawn from multiple sources, including comments made by Nick Tilsen to the Learning/Action Lab in the Regenerative Community Progress Report, November 2014, and in the "Ecosystem of Opportunity: Thunder Valley CDC Documentary," mentioned previously.

14 Neihardt, *Black Elk Speaks*, 151.

15 Bernie Rasmussen, email to Ted Howard and others, February. 28, 2014.

16 Nick Tilsen, interview with Ted Howard, April 17, 2018. Nick Tilsen, "Transition to Amplify Innovation," video, Thunder Valley CDC, aired Feb. 1, 2018 on Vimeo, *https://vimeo.com/253837212.*

17 Bryan Lowry and Katy Bergen, "Sharice Davids Makes History: Kansas' First Gay Rep, 1st Native American Woman in Congress," *Kansas City Star*, November 6, 2018.

18 Stephanie Gutierrez, *An Indigenous Approach to Community Wealth Building: A Lakota Translation* (The Democracy Collaborative, November 2018), 30, *https://democracycollaborative.org/community-wealth-building-a-lakota-translation.*

19 Gutierrez, *An Indigenous Approach*, 27.

20 Daly and Cobb, *For the Common Good*, 5, 8, 161.

21 Winona LaDuke, "Voices from White Earth," in *People, Land, and Community: collected E. F. Schumacher Lectures*, ed. Hildegaard Hannum (New Haven, CT: Yale University Press, 1997), 22–25.

22 Neihardt, *Black Elk Speaks*.

CHAPTER 3

1 Quotes as told to Laura Bliss,"A Portland Startup Is Smashing Barriers to Affordable Housing," City Lab, January 27, 2017, *https://www.citylab.com/solutions/2017/01/a-portland-start-up-is-smashing-barriers-to-affordable-housing/514202/.*

2 Tyrone Poole, interview with Marjorie Kelly and Erin Kesler, May 9, 2017.

3 Alana Samuels, "The Racist History of Portland, the Whitest City in America," *Atlantic*, July 22, 2016.

4 Nikole Hannah-Jones, "Portland Housing Audit Finds Discrimination in 64 Percent of Tests; City Has Yet to Act Against Landlords," *Oregonian*, May 9, 2011, *https://www.oregonlive.com/portland/index.ssf/2011/05/a_portland_housing_audit_finds.html.*

5 Poole, interview with Kelly and Kesler.

6 Kimberly Branam, interview with Marjorie Kelly, January 22, 2015.

7 Anne Mangan, "Sweet News: PDC Launches Startup PDX: Challenge," Oregon Entrepreneurs Network, February 14, 2013, *https://www.oen.org/2013/02/14/sweet-news-pdc-launches-startup-pdxchallenge/*. Portland Development Commission, "PDC Opens 2014 Startup PDX Challenge, Focused on Women and Minorities," PR News Wire, May 21, 2014, *https://www.prnewswire.com/news-releases/pdc-opens-2014-startup-pdx-challenge-focused-on-women--minorities-260094581.html*. The contest ran three years, 2013–2015. Prosper Portland Staff, phone conversation with Sarah Stranahan, December 19, 2018.

8 Prosper Portland, accessed February 14, 2018, *https://prosperportland.us/*.

9 Poole, interview with Kelly and Kesler.

10 Katherine Krajnak, interview with Marjorie Kelly and Erin Kesler, May 10, 2017.

11 Krajnak, interview with Kelly and Kesler.

12 Mark Treskon, "Less Segregated Cities Aren't Only More Inclusive. They're More Prosperous," *Urban Wire: Race and Ethnicity*, Urban Institute, March 28, 2017, *https://www.urban.org/urban-wire/less-segregated-communities-arent-only-more-inclusive-theyre-more-prosperous*.

13 Brandon M. Terry, "MLK Now," essay in "Fifty Years Since MLK," *Boston Review*, 2017, 15.

14 Martin Luther King, Jr., "The Three Evils of Society" speech, Aug. 31, 1967, *https://www.scribd.com/doc/134362247/Martin-Luther-King-Jr-The-Three-Evils-of-Society-1967*.

15 Lisa K. Bates, Ann Curry-Stevens, and Coalition of Communities of Color, *The African-American Community in Multnomah County: An Unsettling Profile* (Portland, OR: Coalition of Communities of Color and Portland State University, 2014), *http://static1.squarespace.com/static/5501f6d4e4b0ee23fb3097ff/t/556d3996e4b09da5e9a521df/1433221526152/African-American-report-FINAL-January-2014.pdf*.

16 Alana Samuels, "The Racist History of Portland, the Whitest City in America," *Atlantic*, July 22, 2016.

17 Samuels, "Racist History of Portland."

18 Nigel Jaquiss, "Critics Blast a Portland Plan to Divert Money Earmarked for the Black Community to Help a Health Care Giant," *Willamette Week*, August 16, 2017, *https://www.wweek.com/news/2017/08/16/critics-blast-a-portland-plan-to-divert-money-earmarked-for-the-black-community-to-help-a-health-care-giant/*.

19 Eliot Neighborhood, "The Hill Block Project Update," February 4, 2018, *https://eliotneighborhood.org/2018/02/04/the-hill-block-project-update/*.

20 Walter Johnson, "To Remake the World: Slavery, Racial Capitalism, and Justice," essay in "Race, Capitalism, Justice," *Boston Review*, Forum 1, 2017, 26–7.

21 Caitlin Rosenthal, "Abolition as Market Regulation," essay in "Race, Capitalism, Justice," *Boston Review*, Forum 1, 2017, 40.

22 "Inclusive Business Resource Network," Prosper Portland, accessed January 6, 2019, *https://prosperportland.us/portfolio-items/inclusive-business-resource-network/*.

23 Local and Regional Government Alliance on Race and Equity, accessed February 11, 2019, *https://www.racialequityalliance.org/*.

24 "Memphis Sanitation Workers' Strike," The Martin Luther King, Jr. Research and Education Institute, Stanford University, accessed February 11, 2019, *https://kinginstitute.stanford.edu/encyclopedia/memphis-sanitation-workers-strike*.

25 Autodidact 17, "Dr. Martin Luther King Jr: 'I fear I am integrating my people into a burning house,'" *New York Amsterdam News*, January 12, 2017, *http://amsterdamnews.com/news/2017/jan/12/dr-martin-luther-king-jr-i-fear-i-am-integrating-m/*.

26 "Portland Housing Startup Snags $2M from Angels," *Portland Business Journal*, December 7, 2018.

CHAPTER 4

1 Daniel, interview with Marjorie Kelly, October 8, 2017. Step Up requested his last name be withheld.

2 Walter Wright, Kathryn W. Hexter, and Nick Downer, "Cleveland's Greater University Circle Initiative: An Anchor-Based Strategy for Change," The Democracy Collaborative, May 2016, 11, *https://democracycollaborative.org/greater-university-circle-initiative*.

3 "2017 Annual Report," Publications, University Hospitals, accessed on February 12, 2019, *https://www.uhhospitals.org/about-uh/publications/corporate-publications/annual-report*.

4 Cleveland Clinic 2017 operating revenue $8.4 billion; Meg Bryant, "Cleveland Clinic 2017 Operating Income, Revenue Bounce Back," Health Care Drive, March 1, 2018, *https://www.healthcaredive.com/news/cleveland-clinic-2017-operating-income-revenue-bounce-back/518134/*. University Hospitals 2017 revenue $3.9 billion; "2017 Annual Report," University Hospitals. Case Western Reserve University (CWRU) 2017 revenue $1 billion; "2016/2017 Annual Report," CWRU, *https://case.edu/behindthestory/images/CWRU-Annual-Report-2017.pdf*.

5 Alexander Kent and Thomas Frolich of 24/7 Wall St., "The 9 Most Segregated Cities in America," *Huffington Post*, Aug. 27, 2015, *https://www.huffingtonpost.com/entry/the-9-most-segregated-cities-in-america_us_55df53e9e4b0e7117ba92d7f*.

6 J. Mark Souther, "Acropolis of the Middle-West: Decay, Renewal, and Boosterism in Cleveland's University Circle," *Journal of Planning History*, 10(1), January 11, 2011, *https://journals.sagepub.com/doi/abs/10.1177/1538513210391892*.

7 Wright, Hexter, and Downer, "Cleveland's Greater University Circle Initiative," 11.

8 Wright, Hexter, and Downer, "Cleveland's Greater University Circle Initiative," 12.

9 Brandon Terry, "A Revolution in Values," essay in "Fifty Years Since MLK," *Boston Review*, 2017, 62.

10 Cleveland's Greater University Circle Initiative: Building a 21st Century City through the Power of Anchor Institution Collaboration, (Cleveland, OH: Cleveland Foundation, 2013), 39, *http://www.clevelandfoundation.org/wp-content/uploads/2014/01/*.

11 Walter Wright, "Greater University Circle Major Accomplishments, 2011–2014," handout, Cleveland State University. Also see Wright, Hexter, and Downer, "Cleveland's Greater University Circle Initiative," 12.

12 John McMicken, email to Ted Howard, January 7, 2019.

13 John McMicken, email to Ted Howard, January 5, 2019.

14 McMicken, email to Howard, January 5, 2019.

15 Healthcare Anchor Network website, Oct. 15, 2018, *https://www.healthcareanchor.network*.

16 "Anchor Collaborative Network," The Democracy Collaborative, accessed February 12, 2019, *http://www.anchorcollabs.org/*. "High Education Anchor Mission Initiative," The Democracy Collaborative, accessed March 17, 2019, *http://anchors.democracycollaborative.org*.

17 Karl Polanyi, *The Great Transformation: The Political and Economic Origins of Our Time* (Boston: Beacon Press, 1960; originally published 1944).

18 See for example, Randy Oostra, "Embracing an Anchor Mission: ProMedica's All-In Strategy," The Democracy Collaborative, May 21, 2018, *https://democracycollaborative.org/content/embracing-anchor-mission-promedica-s-all-strategy*.

19 Tyler Norris and Ted Howard, *Can Hospitals Heal America's Communities?* (Washington, DC: The Democracy Collaborative, December 2015), 12, *https://democracycollaborative.org/content/can-hospitals-heal-americas-communities-0*. "Gross Domestic Product by Industry: Second Quarter 2018," Bureau of Economic Analysis, November 1, 2018, 10–11, *https://www.bea.gov/system/files/2018-10/gdpind218_1.pdf*. Spending by nonprofit hospitals, colleges, and universities at 8.7 percent of GDP is measured by value added.

20 Kim Shelnik and Staci Wampler, interview with Marjorie Kelly, October 8, 2017.

21 Marjorie Kelly, visit to Step Up class, October 9, 2017.

22 Shelnik and Wampler, interview with Kelly. Kim Shelnik, email to Marjorie Kelly, December 20, 2018.

23 Staci Wampler, email to Marjorie Kelly, December 20, 2018.

24 These financial facts are drawn from the annual financial statements of the publicly traded company in question. We have chosen not to reveal the name of this company, which is a prominent employer in the small city of Cleveland.

25 Alex Berenson, *The Number: How the Drive for Quarterly Earnings Corrupted Wall Street and Corporate America* (New York: Random House, 2003), xxviii.

CHAPTER 5

1 Data on home care aide workforce composition from Jay Cassano, "Inside America's Largest Worker-Run Business," *Fast Company*, September 8, 2015.

2 Octaviea Martin quotes from Corinne H. Rieder, Clara Miller, and Jodi M. Sturgeon, "Too Few Good Jobs? Make Bad Jobs Better," *Huffington Post*, Dec. 9, 2012, *https://www.huffingtonpost.com/corinne-h-rieder/make-bad-jobs-better_b_1953051.html*. Octaviea no longer works at CHCA; after taking medical leave, she chose not to return, according to CHCA President Adria Powell, in an interview with Marjorie Kelly, January 2, 2019.

3 CHCA turnover rate of 20–25 percent cited in Marjorie Kelly interview with Michael Elsas, May 25, 2017. Data on industry turnover rate of 66 percent cited in Carlo Calma, "The Big-Picture Strategy to Combatting Caregiver Turnover," *Home Health Care News*, July 30, 2017, *https://homehealthcarenews.com/2017/07/the-big-picture-strategy-to-combatting-caregiver-turnover/*.

4 CHCA, "B Impact Report: Cooperative Home Care Associates (CHCA)," [Best for Overall 2017, Best for Workers 2017, Best for Community 2017, Best for Changemakers 2017], Cooperative Home Care Associates, Certified B Corporation, *https://bcorporation.net/directory/cooperative-home-care-associates-chca*.

5 Ruth Glasser and Jeremy Brecher, *We Are the Roots: The Organizational Culture of a Home Care Cooperative* (Davis, CA: Center for Cooperatives, University of California, 2002), ix.

6 Jack Ewing, "Wages Are Rising in Europe. But Economists are Puzzled," *New York Times*, July 27, 2018.

7 Ewing, "Wages Rising in Europe."

8 Michael Elsas, interview with Marjorie Kelly, May 25, 2017.

9 Caroline Lewis, "The Nation's Largest Worker-Owned Business Is No Longer Just an Experiment in Social Justice," *Crain's New York Business*, January 31, 2017.

10 Adria Powell quote from Lewis, "No Longer Experiment in Social Justice." Quote by Elsas from interview with Kelly, May 25, 2017. CEO pay multiple from Lawrence Mishel and Jessica Schieder, "CEO Pay Remains High Relative to the Pay of Typical Workers and High-Wage Earners," Economic Policy Institute, July 20, 2017, *https://www.epi.org/publication/ceo-pay-remains-high-relative-to-the-pay-of-typical-workers-and-high-wage-earners/*.

11 Elsas, interview with Kelly.

12 Glasser and Brecher, *We Are the Roots*, 4. Elsas, interview with Kelly.

13 Anne Inserra, Maureen Conway, and John Rodat, "The Cooperative Home Care Associates, Sectoral Employment Development Learning Project," Aspen Institute Economic Opportunities Program, Washington, DC, February 2002, 18–19.

14 Adria Powell, interview with Marjorie Kelly, January 2, 2019.

15 Glasser and Brecher, *We Are the Roots*, 9.

16 Glasser and Brecher, *We Are the Roots*, 84.

17 Inserra, Conway, and Rodat, "Cooperative Home Care Associates," 38.

18 Inserra, Conway, and Rodat," Cooperative Home Care Associates," 23.

19 Charlie Sabatino and Caroleigh Newman, "The New Status of Home Care Workers Under the Fair Labor Standards Act," *Bifocal: A Journal of the Commission on Law and Aging*, American Bar Association 36, 6 (July–August 2015), *https://www.americanbar.org/content/dam/aba/publications/bifocal/BIFOCALJuly-August2015.pdf*.

20 Powell, interview with Kelly. Rick Surpin, emails to Marjorie Kelly, December 20, 2018, January 28, 2019, January 29, 2019.

21 Chris Farrell, "Could This Idea Help Fix America's Shortage of Home Care Workers?" *Forbes*, August 15, 2017.

22 David Hammer of ICA Group, interview with Marjorie Kelly, July 8, 2017. Amy Baxter, "AARP Foundation Funds Project to Explore Home Care Cooperative Sustainability," *Home Health Care News*, March 22, 2017. Home Care Cooperative Initiative, website of Cooperative Development Foundation, accessed February 12, 2019, *http://seniors.coop/*.

23 Eduardo Porter, "Home Health Care: Shouldn't It Be Work Worth Doing?" *New York Times*, August 29, 2017. Hammer, interview with Kelly.

24 "Investor Relations: Financing America's Electric Cooperatives," National Rural Utilities Cooperative Finance Corporation, accessed February 12, 2019, *https://www.nrucfc.coop/content/nrucfc/en/investor-relations.html*.

25 Tim McMahon, "Current U-6 Unemployment Rate," UnemploymentData.com, January 4, 2019, *https://unemploymentdata.com/current-u6-unemployment-rate/*. Charles Jeszeck, "Contingent Workforce: Size, Characteristics, Earnings, and Benefits," US Government Accountability Office, May 2015.

26 GAO, "Contingent Workforce: Size, Characteristics, Earnings, and Benefits," US Government Accountability Office, April 20, 2015, *https://www.gao.gov/assets/670/669766.pdf*.

27 Research by economists Thomas Piketty, Emmanuel Saez, and Gabriel Zucman, reported by Patricia Cohen, "A Bigger Economic Pie, but a Smaller Slice for Half of the U.S.," *New York Times*, December 6, 2016.

28 Nick Hanauer, "Stock Buybacks Are Killing the American Economy," *Atlantic*, February 5, 2015.

29 Data source US Department of Commerce, Bureau of Economic Analysis combined charts (Gross Domestic Product; Gross Domestic Income: Compensation of Employees, Paid: Wages and Salaries; Corporate Profits after Tax [without IVA and CCAdj]), retrieved from FRED, Federal Reserve Bank of St. Louis, February 25, 2019, *https://myf.red/g/n0s9*. Recreating and updating chart done by Derek Thompson, "Corporate Profits Are Eating the Economy," *Atlantic*, March 4, 2013, *http://www.theatlantic.com/business/archive/2013/03/corporate-profits-are-eating-the-economy/273687/*.

30 Derek Thompson, "A World Without Work," *Atlantic*, July/August 2015.

31 Thomas Paine, "The Rights of Man," in *Paine: Collected Writings* (New York: Library of America, 1995), 465.

32 E. F. Schumacher, "Buddhist Economics," in *Small Is Beautiful: Economics as If People Mattered* (Vancouver, BC: Hartley and Marks Publishers, 1999 [copyright 1973]), 38.

33 Schumacher, "Buddhist Economics," 38–39.

34 Glasser and Brecher, *We Are the Roots*, 98–99.

35 Glasser and Brecher, *We Are the Roots*, 102.

36 Ronnie Galvin, "Confronting Our Common Enemy: Elite White Male Supremacy," *Medium*, February 4, 2017, *https://medium.com/@ronniegalvin/confronting-our-common-enemy-6f923f74cb3b*.

37 Powell, interview with Kelly.

38 Powell, interview with Kelly.

39 Powell, interview with Kelly.

40 Powell, interview with Kelly.

CHAPTER 6

1 Robert Heilbroner, *The Limits of American Capitalism* (New York: Harper and Row, 1965).

2 Mike Chanov, interview with Marjorie Kelly and Erin Kesler, March 2, 2017.

3 Jay Apperson, "Power Company to Pay $1 Million Penalty, Perform $1 Million in Environmental Projects, Upgrade Water Pollution-Prevention Technology," Department of the Environment, Maryland.gov, *https://news.maryland.gov/mde/2016/08/29/power-company-to-pay-1-million-penalty-perform-1-million-in-environmental-projects-upgrade-water-pollution-prevention-technology/*.

4 Loren Jensen, interview with Marjorie Kelly, April 25, 2017.

5 William Rue, interview with Marjorie Kelly, March 2, 2017.

6 Ian MacFarlane and Peter Ney, interview with Marjorie Kelly, December 2, 2016.

7 "Peter Ney Recognized as a Top Chief Financial Officer by Baltimore Business Journal," press release, *EA in the News*, EA Engineering, April 21, 2015, *https://eaest.com/articles_news/2015_04_21_Ney_Top_CFO.php*.

8 MacFarlane and Ney, December 2, 2016.

9 David Kiron, Nina Kruschwitz, Holger Rubel, Martin Reeves, and Sonja-Katrin Fuisz-Kehrbach, "Sustainability's Next Frontier: Walking the Talk on the Sustainability Issues That Matter the Most," *The MIT Sloan Management Review*, December 16, 2013, *https://sloanreview.mit.edu/projects/sustainabilitys-next-frontier/*.

10 Carina Millstone, *Frugal Value* (New York: Routledge, 2017), 135–145, 147–162.

11 Bill Rue, email to Marjorie Kelly, September 18, 2018.

12 Dan Fagin, *Toms River* (Washington, DC: Island Press, 2013), 13, 131–132, 138.

13 Fagin, *Toms River*, 145, 154, 155, 189.

14 Fagin, *Toms River*, 223.

15 Franklin Roosevelt, campaign address at Chicago, October 14, 1936.

16 "The Servant as Leader," Robert K. Greenleaf Center for Servant Leadership, website, accessed October 2, 2018, *https://www.greenleaf.org/what-is-servant-leadership/*.

17 "Laws, Mandates, and Ordinances Requiring LEED," Everblue, April 5, 2018, *www.everbluetraining.com/blog/laws-mandates-and-ordinances-requiring-leed*.

18 Joseph Blasi and Douglas Kruse, "Small Business Owners Are Getting a New Incentive to Sell to Their Employees," *The Conversation*, August 15, 2018, *https://theconversation.com/small-business-owners-are-getting-a-new-incentive-to-sell-to-their-employees-101515*.

19 NCEO, *Employee Ownership and Economic Well-Being* (Oakland, CA: National Center for Employee Ownership, May 15, 2017), *https://www.ownershipeconomy.org/*.

20 "Small Business Closure Crisis," Project Equity, accessed October 6, 2018, *https://www.project-equity.org/communities/small-business-closure-crisis/*.

21 Fifty by Fifty, accessed February 16, 2019, *https://www.fiftybyfifty.org/*.

22 Ian MacFarlane, interview with Marjorie Kelly, September 27, 2018.

CHAPTER 7

1 Winona LaDuke, *All Our Relations: Native Struggles for Land and Life* (Chicago: Haymarket Books, 1999), 199. Proposed amendment to US Constitution by Walt Bresette et al., "Seventh Generation Amendment," Anishinaabe Niijii flyer, Bayfield, WI, March 1996.

2 Carla Santos Skandier, interview with Marjorie Kelly, October 8, 2018.

3 Climate Breakthrough Project, "Big Strategies. Talented Leaders. Global Impact," accessed February 16, 2019, *https://www.climatebreakthroughproject.org/*.

4 David Roberts, "This Graphic Explains Why 2 Degrees of Global Warming Will Be Way Worse than 1.5," *Vox*, October 7, 2018, *https://www.vox.com/energy-and-environment/2018/1/19/16908402/global-warming-2-degrees-climate-change*.

5 Reed Landberg, Chisaki Watanabe, and Heesu Lee, "Climate Crisis Spurs UN Call for $2.4 Trillion Fossil Fuel Shift," *Bloomberg*, October 7, 2018. Chris Mooney and Brady Dennis, "The World Has Just Over a Decade to Get Climate Change Under Control, U.N. Scientists Say," *Washington Post*, October 7, 2018.

6 Landberg et al., "Climate Crisis Spurs Call."

7 "Despite the Paris Agreement, Governments Still Give Billions in Fossil Fuel Finance Each Year," Oil Change International, November 2017, *https://priceofoil.org/content/uploads/2017/11/SFF_COP23_infographic.pdf*.

8 Andrew Bary, "Exxon Mobil Is a Bet on the Future of Oil," *Barron's*, May 5, 2018, *https://www.barrons.com/articles/exxon-mobil-is-a-bet-on-the-future-of-oil-1525482562*.

9 Bill McKibben, "Global Warming's Terrifying New Math," *Rolling Stone*, July 19, 2012.

10 Kate Aranoff, "With a Green New Deal, Here's What the World Could Look Like for the Next Generation," *The Intercept*, December 5, 2018, *https://theintercept.com/2018/12/05/green-new-deal-proposal-impacts/*.

11 Editorial Board, "Wake Up World Leaders. The Alarm Is Deafening," Opinion, *New York Times*, October 9, 2018.

12 Suzanne Goldenberg, "Tea Party Climate Change Deniers Funded by BP and Other Major Polluters," *The Guardian*, October 24, 2010. John Cushman Jr., "Harvard Study Finds Exxon Misled Public about Climate Change," *Inside Climate News*, August 22, 2017, *https://insideclimatenews.org/news/22082017/study-confirms-exxon-misled-public-about-climate-change-authors-say*; "Koch Industries: Secretly Funding the Climate Denial Machine," Greenpeace, accessed October 14, 2018, *https://www.greenpeace.org/usa/global-warming/climate-deniers/koch-industries/*.

13 Bill McKibben, "Up Against Big Oil in the Midterms," *New York Times*, November 7, 2018.

14 McKibben, "Up Against Big Oil."

15 Gar Alperovitz, Joe Guinan, and Thomas M. Hanna, "The Policy Weapon Climate Activists Need," *The Nation*, April 26, 2017. Jeff Cox, "$12 Trillion of QE and the Lowest Rates in 5,000 Years … for This?" *CNBC Finance*, June 13, 2016.

16 Alexander Barkawi, "Why Monetary Policy Should Be Green," *Financial Times*, May 18, 2017. Jack Ewing, "Europeans Fear a Global Slump," *New York Times*, March 8, 2019.

17 Marc Labonte, *Monetary Policy and the Federal Reserve: Current Policy and Conditions* (Washington, DC: Congressional Research Service, Jan. 28, 2016).

18 Ben Bernanke, interview with CBS News, December 2010, quoted in Ann Pettifor, *Just Money: How Society Can Break the Despotic Power of Finance* (London: Commonwealth, 2014).

19 Pierre Monin and Alexander Barkawi, "Monetary Policy and Green Financing: Exploring the Links," chapter 7 in *Greening China's Financial System* (Canada: International

Institute for Sustainable Development, 2015), *https://www.iisd.org/library/greening-chinas-financial-system*. Richard Murphy and Colin Hines, *Green Quantitative Easing: Paying for the Economy We Need* (Norfolk, UK: Finance for the Future, 2010), *https://www.financeforthefuture.com/GreenQuEasing.pdf*.

20 Barkawi, "Monetary Policy Should Go Green."

21 Market value, "The World's Largest Public Companies," *Forbes*, 2018, *https://www.forbes.com/global2000/list/*.

22 Alperovitz, Guinan, and Hanna, "Policy Weapon Activists Need."

23 Aldo Leopold, *A Sand County Almanac* (New York: Oxford University Press, 1966), x.

24 Leopold, *Sand County Almanac*, 219–220.

25 Leopold, *Sand County Almanac*, 230.

26 Julian Brave NoiseCat, "The Western Idea of Private Property Is Flawed. Indigenous Peoples Have It Right," *The Guardian*, March 27, 2017.

27 BBC News, "India's Ganges and Yumana Rivers Are 'Not Living Entities,' *BBC News*, July 7, 2017, *https://www.bbc.com/news/world-asia-india-40537701*.

28 SeventhFireBlog, "Unto the Seventh Generation," People of the Seventh Fire, accessed January 3, 2019, *https://seventhfireblog.wordpress.com/2017/03/05/unto-the-seventh-generation/*.

29 Alperovitz, Guinan, and Hanna, "Policy Weapon Activists Need."

30 Mark Carney, governor of the Bank of England, chairman of the Financial Stability Board, "Breaking the Tragedy of the Horizon—Climate Change and Financial Stability," speech to Lloyd's of London, September 29, 2015, *https://www.fsb.org/wp-content/uploads/Breaking-the-Tragedy-of-the-Horizon-%E2%80%93-climate-change-and-financial-stability.pdf*.

31 Adam Vaughn, "Global Demand for Fossil Fuels Will Peak in 2023, Says Thinktank," *Guardian*, September 11, 2018.

32 Dominique Mosbergen, "One of America's Oldest Coal Companies Just Filed for Bankruptcy," *Huffington Post*, October 10, 2018.

33 "Energy" sector performance, Fidelity, accessed January 3, 2019, *https://eresearch.fidelity.com/eresearch/markets_sectors/sectors/sectors_in_market.jhtml?tab=learn§or=10*. "S&P 500 Historical Annual Returns," Macrotrends, *https://www.macrotrends.net/2526/sp-500-historical-annual-returns*.

34 Pilita Clark, "Mark Carney Warns Investors Face 'Huge' Climate Change Losses," *Financial Times*, September 29, 2015.

35 Gar Alperovitz, interview with Marjorie Kelly, September 13, 2018.

36 "Time to Buy Out Fossil Fuel Corporations—Gar Alperovitz on Reality Asserts Itself," Gar Alperovitz, interview with *Real News Network*, April 28, 2017, *https://therealnews.com/stories/galperovitz0421rai*.

CHAPTER 8

1 Matthew Brown, interview with Marjorie Kelly, October 22, 2018. Aditya Chakrabortty, "In 2011 Preston Hit Rock Bottom. Then It Took Back Control," *Guardian*, January 31, 2018.

2 Brown, interview with Kelly.

3 Clifford Singer, "The Preston Model," *The Next System Project* (Washington, DC: The Democracy Collaborative, September 9, 2016).

4 Matthew Brown, PowerPoint presentation to The Democracy Collaborative, October 22, 2018.

5 George Eaton, "How Preston—the UK's 'Most Improved City'—Became a Success Story for Corbynomics," *New Statesman*, November 1, 2018.

6 "Building the Democratic Economy, from Preston to Cleveland," *Laura Flanders Show*, June 24, 2018, *https://therealnews.com/stories/laura-flanders-show-building-the-democratic-economy-from-preston-to-cleveland%E2%80%8B*.

7 "Preston, Jeremy Corbyn's Model Town: How One City Became an Unlikely Laboratory for Corbynomics," *Economist*, October 19, 2017.

8 Labour Party, "For the Many Not the Few," *Labour Party Manifesto 2017, https://labour.org.uk/wp-content/uploads/2017/10/labour-manifesto-2017.pdf*.

9 Kate Aranoff, "Is Nationalization an Answer to Climate Change?" *Intercept*, September 8, 2018, *https://theintercept.com/2018/09/08/jeremy-corbyn-labour-climate-change/*. Eaton, "How Preston Became Success Story."

10 Peter Walker and Jessica Elgot, "Corbyn Defies Doubters as Labour Gains Seats," *Guardian*, June 9, 2017, *https://www.theguardian.com/politics/2017/jun/09/jeremy-corbyn-labour-defies-doubters-gain-seats-election-2017*.

11 Christine Berry, *Towards a People's Banking System: New Thinking for the British Economy* (Commonwealth Publishing, 2018), *http://commonwealth-publishing.com/shop/new-thinking-for-the-british-economy/*. Natalya Naqvi, "Labour's Investment Bank Plan Could Help Fix *Our* Damaging Financial System," *New Statesman*, May 17, 2017.

12 Laura Flanders, "In the Age of Disaster Capitalism, Is 'Survival Socialism' the Solution?" *Nation*, July 19, 2018. Hazel Sheffield, "The Preston Model: UK Takes Lessons in Recovery from Rust-Belt Cleveland," *Guardian*, April 11, 2017.

13 Lawrence White and Andrew MacAskill, "British Banks Set to Close Record 762 Branches This Year," *Reuters*, August 23, 2017, *https://uk.reuters.com/article/uk-britain-banks-branches-idUKKCN1B31AY*.

14 Brown, interview with Kelly. "Sparkassen Savings Banks in Germany," Centre for Public Impact, March 27, 2017, *https://www.centreforpublicimpact.org/case-study/sparkassen-savings-banks-germany/*.

15 Tony Greenham, "Everyone a Banker? Welcome to the New Co-operative Banking Movement," RSA, June 30, 2017.

16 Jules Peck, "Building a Bank That Puts People before Profit," *Business West,* February 20, 2018, *https://www.businesswest.co.uk/blog/building-bank-puts-people-profit.*

17 Natalya Naqvi, "Labour's Investment Bank Plan Could Help Fix Our Damaging Financial System," *New Statesman,* May 17, 2017.

18 Legislative initiatives, Public Banking Institute, accessed November 6, 2018, *https://www.publicbankinginstitute.org/legislative.*

19 Jane Jacobs, *The Death and Life of Great American Cities* (New York: Random House, 1961), 4.

20 Jane Jacobs, *The Nature of Economies* (New York: Random House, 2000).

21 Kevin Phillips, *American Theocracy: The Peril and Politics of Radical Religion, Oil, and Borrowed Money in the 21st Century* (New York: Viking Penguin, 2006), 265–268.

22 Phillips, *American Theocracy,* 265–268.

23 Analysis by Howard Reed, Director Landman Economics, UK, for The Democracy Collaborative. Data source: UK Office for National Statistics, "United Kingdom National Accounts: The Blue Book 2018."

24 Marjorie Kelly, "Overload," chap. 4 in *Owning Our Future: The Emerging Ownership Revolution* (San Francisco: Berrett-Koehler, 2012) 65–83.

25 Howard Reed, emails to Joe Guinan and Marjorie Kelly, January 7, 2019. Data source: Office for National Statistics, UK Statistics Authority (2018).

26 Analysis Reed for The Democracy Collaborative.

27 Jon Craig, "Shadow Chancellor John McDonnell Targets Government's North-South Funding Gap," *Sky News,* February 4, 2017, *https://news.sky.com/story/shadow-chancellor-john-mcdonnell-targets-governments-north-south-funding-gap-10755206.*

28 Richard Partington, "IMF Warns Storm Clouds Are Gathering for Next Financial Crisis," *Guardian,* December 11, 2018. Alex Williams, "Are You Ready for the Financial Crisis of 2019?" *New York Times,* December 10, 2018.

29 Thomas M. Hanna, *The Crisis Next Time: Planning for Public Ownership as an Alternative to Corporate Bank Bailouts* (Washington, DC: The Democracy Collaborative, 2018). Berry, "Toward People's Banking System.

30 Impact Entrepreneur Network, *https://impactalchemist.com/?ss_source=sscampaigns&ss_campaign_id=5c33592d6d86dd0001f41537&ss_email_id=5c336567fbd67200016db664&ss_campaign_name=Live+Webinars+on+Opportunity+Zones+and+The+Clean+Money+Revolution%21&ss_campaign_sent_date=2019-01-07T14%3A42%3A47Z.*

31 Jade Hemeon, "Millennials, Women Drive Trend Toward Responsible Investing," *Investment Executive,* June 6, 2016, *https://www.investmentexecutive.com/news/industry-news/millennials-women-drive-trend-toward-responsible-investing/.*

32 Eilee Anzilotti, "This New Fund Will Help Retiring Baby Boomers Turn Their Businesses into Worker Co-ops," *Fast Company*, November 13, 2018.

33 Richard May, Robert Hockett, and Christopher Mackin, "Encouraging Inclusive Growth: The Employee Equity Loan Act," unpublished paper, presented at Beyster Symposium, Rutgers University, June 2018.

34 Brown, interview with Kelly.

CONCLUSION

1 Donella Meadows, *Leverage Points: Places to Intervene in a System* (Hartland, VT: The Sustainability Institute, 1999), *https://www.donellameadows.org/wp-content/userfiles/Leverage_Points.pdf*.

2 Meadows, *Leverage Points*.

3 George Lakoff, interview with Marjorie Kelly, August 24, 2006.

4 John Schwartz, "Rockefellers, Heirs to an Oil Fortune, Will Divest Charity of Fossil Fuels," *New York Times*, September 21, 2014, *https://www.nytimes.com/2014/09/22/us/heirs-to-an-oil-fortune-join-the-divestment-drive.html*.

5 Damian Carrington, "Ireland Becomes World's First Country to Divest from Fossil Fuels," *Guardian*, July 12, 2018, *https://www.theguardian.com/environment/2018/jul/12/ireland-becomes-worlds-first-country-to-divest-from-fossil-fuels*. Bill McKibben, "A Future without Fossil Fuels," *New York Review of Books*, April 4, 2019.

6 AmalgamatedBank, "Move Your Money," *https://www.moveyourmoney.com/*.

7 Edgar Villanueva, *Decolonizing Wealth* (San Francisco: Berrett-Koehler, 2018), *http://decolonizingwealth.com/*.

8 Marjorie Kelly and Sarah Stranahan, "Next Generation Enterprise Design," Democracy Collaborative, November 7, 2018, *https://medium.com/fifty-by-fifty/next-generation-enterprise-design-the-employee-owned-benefit-corporation-7b5001f8f1a8*. A convening was also held April 29, 2019, bringing together employee-owned benefit corporations and B Corporations.

9 Dana Brown, "Before Big Pharma Kills Us, Maybe Public Pharma Can Save Us," *The American Prospect*, Aug. 27, 2018, *https://prospect.org/article/big-pharma-kills-us-maybe-public-pharma-can-save-us*.

10 Gar Alperovitz, "Technological Inheritance and the Case for a Basic Income," Economic Security Project, December 16, 2016, *https://medium.com/economicsecproj/technological-inheritance-and-the-case-for-a-basic-income-ded373a69c8e*, Gar Alperovitz and Lew Daly, *Unjust Desserts: How the Rich are Taking Our Common Inheritance and Why We Should Take It Back* (New York: New Press, 2008), *https://www.garalperovitz.com/unjust-deserts/*.

11 Meadows, *Leverage Points*.

ACKNOWLEDGMENTS

Many minds and many hands go into the work of building the democratic economy, without whom this book and our work would not be possible. We owe a special debt to Gar Alperovitz for his vision for The Democracy Collaborative and the next system. We're grateful to publisher Steve Piersanti for his encouragement and for pushing our prose toward greater clarity and directness, to copyeditor Rebecca Rider for her impeccable review and fine-tuning, to Maureen Forys for an elegant interior design, and to all the Berrett-Koehler staff for being fabulous to work with. We also offer deepest gratitude to Naomi Klein and Aditya Chakrabortty for generously agreeing to grace these pages with their elegant foreword and afterword. A warm thanks from Marjorie to Sarah Stranahan, who was there assisting with research from the very start, and with checking facts at the very end; you're a gem, Sarah, and a dear friend. Isaiah Poole made the introduction sing with his skillful, brilliant edits, and generously rescued this manuscript in many other ways. Karen Kahn's masterful changes to the title were a godsend.

Warmest thanks to all those we visit, interview, and quote in this book, whose work is the substance of it all. At the Evergreen Cooperatives, thanks to John McMicken and Brett Jones for how they continue to grow and evolve these vital businesses modeling a democratic economy, a beacon to so many. Also hats off to our colleague Jessica Rose for her work with Brett and John on the creation of the Fund for Employee Ownership; you're all taking Evergreen's work to inspiring new levels. For Ted, helping in the development of Evergreen was a highlight of a lifetime, working arm in arm with India Pierce Lee, Ronn Richard, Lillian Kuri, and all the anchor leaders and the business development team, including Tracey Nichols. Special thanks, too, to Chris Brown for sharing news of his path, and to Dale Maharidge for making us aware of Chris.

Evergreen and The Democracy Collaborative itself wouldn't haven't happened without our former colleague Steve Dubb, whose wisdom and insights shine through every page of this book. Both of us and the whole organization are so grateful to you, Steve.

We thank all the participants in the Learning/Action Lab for giving us the kick in the pants we needed and teaching us about co-learning and co-creation. Kisses to Sarah McKinley and Jill Bamburg for leading that life-changing project, and making sure we had fun along the way. Huge thanks to Justin Huenemann and Karla Miller for setting it all in motion. We have the most profound admiration for Nick Tilsen, Karlene Hunter, Mark Tilsen, Sharice Davids, Jo White, and others we met at Thunder Valley and on Pine Ridge; we feel privileged to have walked with you. Rae Tall, Stephanie Gutierrez, and Kristen Wagner of Hope Nation, thank you for the gift of your Lakota translation and embrace of community wealth building.

We're grateful for Tyrone Poole, Kimberly Branam, Katherine Krajnak, and other staffers of Prosper Portland who graciously took time with us to share their insights, and to review the chapter in draft form. Thanks to Erin Kesler for research and drafting assistance on this chapter and her leadership of a memorable trip to Portland. In Cleveland, many thanks to Daniel, Kim Shelnik, Staci Wampler, and Yvette Herod for welcoming Marjorie so warmly. And a shout-out to The Democracy Collaborative board member Walter Wright for his care in commenting on this chapter and his leadership of GUCI.

Our CHCA visit and research was rewarding, thanks to Adria Powell, Michael Elsas, Rick Surpin, and Peggy Powell. Warm thanks to our colleague Ronnie Galvin for his wisdom, which caps off this chapter nicely.

To our new friends at EA Engineering, Loren Jensen, Ian MacFarlane, Mike Chanov, Bill Rue, Peter Ney, Barb Roeper, and Erin Toothaker—it's been a blast getting to know you and your incredible company. Can we come work there? Warmest thanks to our colleague Carla Santos

Skandier and the funders of the Climate Breakthrough Project for leadership on the breakthrough idea of QE for the planet. Big hug to Johanna Bozuwa for taking that chapter in hand and polishing it. Special thanks to Thomas Hanna for his fast work in pinpointing accurate key statistics, which he seems to keep at the ready in his pockets every moment.

For the Preston chapter, huge admiration to the astonishing person of Matthew Brown, and warm thanks to everyone Ted has been meeting there, including John McDonnell, Jeremy Corbyn, Jules Peck, Neil McInroy, and others at CLES and the New Economics Foundation. Howard Reed of Landman Economics, you bailed us out of a tight data spot at the last minute, and Marjorie owes you a pint. For Joe Guinan, no thanks are enough for who you are, but a special tip of the hat for providing the intellectual frame for the ethical finance chapter—and for your brilliant leadership in our organization. Others for whom we are grateful include Dick May of American Working Capital and Joseph Blasi for their research and ideas on employee ownership. Also warm thanks to Sandy Wiggins, BALLE, and RSF Social Finance, Kelly Ryan of Incourage Foundation, and all the community foundation leaders Marjorie got to know at that first CF Circle.

Members of our board of trustees are deeply woven in our work, and in this book. Stephanie McHenry made one of the first loans to Evergreen. Allan Henderson helped with the title, and also pushed us to uncover what was missing in our earlier analysis. Dayna Cunningham and Tamara Copeland offered generous board training that deepened our understanding of race, which they'll find reflected in this book. Mary Emeny, Walter Wright, and Charles McNeil have supported The Democracy Collaborative in many ways, including with thoughtful comments on this work in progress.

The work of The Democracy Collaborative wouldn't be possible without our funders, including these individuals and foundations: Diane Ives, Diana Blank, and Dena Kimball of Kendeda; Peter and Jennifer Buffett of NoVo; Leslie Harroun of Partners for a New Economy; Phil Henderson and Shawn Escoffery of Surdna; Loren Harris and Taina McField of Nathan Cummings; Charles Rutheiser of Annie E. Casey; India Pierce Lee, Lillian Kuri, and Ronn Richard of the Cleveland Foundation; Laurie and Julie Schecter of Shift; Karla Miller of Northwest Area; David Bright and Robin Varghese of Open Society; Darryl Young of Summit; Jeanne Wardford of Kellogg; Dana Bezerra and Amy Orr of Heron; Beth Versten and Brittany Andersen of New Visions; Mariah McPherson of New Belgium Family Foundation; Amy Slonim and Paul Tarini of Robert Wood Johnson; Chris Kabel and Katie Byerly of Kresge, plus other generous organizations and individuals.

John Duda has shepherded this process in more ways than we can count, in addition to being the most productive human being on the face of the earth. Dana Brown, thanks for the great addition on public pharma, so timely, and for all your work on Next System. Hats off to Peter Gowan for important new research on Inclusive Ownership Funds. Much appreciation to Adam Simpson for help in thinking what's next with technology and jobs in a next system. Deepest gratitude to Katrina Bukovac, who makes all our work possible, and does so with limitless grace and poise. And Rhonda Coleman, what would we do without you, lady?

We wish also to thank key people in the field with whom we have worked and from whom we have learned what we know, including Melissa Hoover, Camille Kerr, Ira Harkavy, Randy Royster, Ashleigh Gardere, Gary Cohen, Tyler Norris, Deborah Ellwood, Michelline Davis; Hilary Abell and Alison Lingane of Project Equity; Mikel Lezamiz and Ander Exteberria of Mondragon; David Korten and Fran Korten of Yes!; Thad Williamson, Reggie Gordon, and Evette Roots from Richmond; Lovely Warren, Henry Fitts, and Kate Washington from Rochester; Angela Glover Blackwell from PolicyLink; Denise Fairchild and Tara Marchant from Emerald Cities; Repa Mekha, Elena Gaardere, and Theresa Gardella from Nexus Community Partners; Lee Anne Adams, Geraldine Gardner, Lucy Kerman, Kurt Somers, Patrick Horvath, and Carla Javits.

Many thanks to those who gave a careful reading to an early draft and offered valuable critiques, including Tom Kruse, Michelle Lam, Sarah Modlin, Shonali Banerjee, and Meera Velu. And a final thanks to Shelley Alpern for her reading of the manuscript, her impeccable grammar, and her patience (most of the time) during the long disappearance that was the writing of this book.

INDEX

C

P

Y

ABOUT THE AUTHORS

Marjorie Kelly, Executive Vice President, The Democracy Collaborative

Marjorie Kelly, lead author on this book, is executive vice president at The Democracy Collaborative and a nationally recognized expert in enterprise and financial design for social mission. She comes from a business family, where her father owned a small business and her grandfather founded Anderson Tool and Die in Chicago. Her social activism began at Earlham College, where she studied English and protested the Vietnam War. While pursuing a master's in journalism at the University of Missouri, her real political awakening occurred with the discovery of feminism. It was an eye-opening exercise in questioning received wisdom and recognizing invisible bias, which informed her later concept of capital bias, explored for the first time in this book.

A youthful enthusiasm for collectives was tempered as she served as president of the board of Williamson Street Grocery Cooperative in Madison, Wisconsin, at a time when sales doubled. Marjorie helped initiate a shift to differential pay at that cooperative where the manager of the $1 million operation was paid the same as a person hired a week earlier to stock shelves.

Marjorie co-founded *Business Ethics* magazine, known for its listing of the "100 Best Corporate Citizens," Russell 1000 firms excelling at serving multiple stakeholders, not just stockholders. Over 20 years as president of that publishing company, she watched the corporate social and environmental responsibility fields grow, even as corporate practices worsened, with corporations initiating massive layoffs, fighting unions, ending traditional pensions, and moving operations overseas to evade regulation. She had started the publication believing good business people could change the world, but she saw how even CEOs are powerless against the real force in the system, Wall Street's mandate for perpetually growing profits. She explored this analysis in *The Divine Right of Capital,* named one of *Library Journal*'s 10 Best Business Books of 2001.

In search of solutions, Marjorie joined Tellus Institute, a Boston think tank, where with Allen White (cofounder of the Global Reporting Initiative), she cofounded Corporation 20/20, gathering hundreds of leaders from business, finance, law, labor, and civil society to explore corporate design that integrates social, ecological, and financial aims. She consulted to the Ford Foundation's WealthWorks project, developing innovations in rural development for the Deep South and Appalachia, later serving on a rural policy council for Senator Bernie Sanders. Marjorie worked with Cutting Edge Capital, doing hands-on design for social mission for private company clients. She published *Owning Our Future: The Emerging Ownership Revolution* and has also written for publications including *Harvard Business Review, New England Law Review, Chief Executive, Stanford Social Innovation Review,* and the *San Francisco Chronicle.*

At The Democracy Collaborative, Marjorie has worked on projects from aiding community foundations with place-based impact investing to working with Native American leaders on inclusive development. With Jessica Rose and others, she cofounded the Fifty by Fifty initiative to help catalyze 50 million worker-owners by 2050, perceiving that employee ownership is the democratic economy model most ready for scale. She lives in Salem, Massachusetts, with her wife Shelley Alpern.

Ted Howard, President, The Democracy Collaborative

Ted Howard's road to becoming an internationally sought-after expert in the reconstruction of equitable local economies and strategies for building community wealth has been a long and winding one. Born in Ohio, he grew up in Los Angeles in the 1960s, spending much of his time body surfing in Santa Monica and taking advantage of his nearly seven-foot-tall frame on the basketball court. He headed to Washington, DC, in September of 1968 to attend the Georgetown University School of Foreign Service with the intention of becoming an American diplomat—but wound up majoring in anti-war organizing instead. After the shootings at Kent State and Jackson State, he helped pull off the May 1970 student strike that shut down Georgetown for the first time since its founding in 1789, and, realizing the moral bankruptcy of a career in the Vietnam-era State Department, he dropped out of Georgetown, moved back to California, and threw himself into organizing, helping galvanize so much opposition to President Nixon's planned 1972 GOP convention in San Diego that they moved it at the last minute to Miami Beach on the other side of the country.

Back on the East Coast, he began working with Jeremy Rifkin as co-director of the Peoples Bicentennial Commission, a radical alternative to the Nixon/Ford celebrations planned for 1976. With Rifkin, he co-authored a number of books on emerging technological developments and economic alternatives before switching gears in the 1980s to work with several UN agencies and The Hunger Project on poverty and international development, spending time in India and Africa. While working abroad, Howard's exposure to traditional communal models and post-colonial experiments confirmed his intuition that extractive corporate capitalism was far from the only way to organize an economic system. Bringing this perspective back in the 1990s to the US, Howard connected with historian and political economist Gar Alperovitz, first as the executive director of Alperovitz's National Center for Economic Alternatives, then as cofounders in 2000 of The Democracy Collaborative.

At The Democracy Collaborative, where Howard currently serves as president, he helped design and oversee the implementation of Cleveland's Evergreen Cooperatives, a pathbreaking experiment in inclusive local economic development that leverages the purchasing power of local anchor institutions like hospitals and universities to foster democratic ownership of industry, benefiting some of the city's most excluded and marginalized communities. His commitment to this project, and his belief that the most promising solutions for a better future often find more fertile soil in the places left behind by the present, brought him back to Ohio in 2007, where he continues to reside today. Identified in the *Guardian* as "the de facto spokesperson for community wealth building" internationally, Howard's expertise in transformative local economic development has been sought out by leading healthcare systems and universities and city governments from Albuquerque to Amsterdam, multiple regional branches of the Federal Reserve system, the British Labour Party, and England's Royal Society of Arts.

The Democracy Collaborative

The Democracy Collaborative is a research and development lab for the democratic economy. Celebrating its 20th anniversary in 2020, The Democracy Collaborative was launched as a special initiative at the University of Maryland by cofounders Ted Howard and Gar Alperovitz. The organization now is an independent nonprofit that has grown into a national and international hub for the development and implementation of transformative economic solutions. Its staff of 40 is based predominantly in Washington, DC, and Cleveland, Ohio, with other staff and fellows in places like Boston; Preston, England; and Brussels, Belgium. We work in theory, policy, and practice to create models and strategies for a community-sustaining economy.

The Democracy Collaborative works for systems change in the political economy, designing models and strategies that address the drivers causing the crises that make the headlines. The organization was one of the architects and codevelopers of Cleveland's Evergreen Cooperatives, a network of three employee-owned companies supported by purchasing from large anchor institutions, such as nonprofit hospitals and universities. That model is one example of a community wealth building approach to local economic development, using strategies around worker cooperatives, community land trusts, and other forms of democratic and community ownership. This approach, pioneered by The Democracy Collaborative, has begun to move decisively into the toolbox of municipal governments and community advocates. Key to this framework is developing existing place-based assets—especially those of large nonprofit anchor institutions—to support and scale inclusive local economic development that benefits the disadvantaged.

Beyond the neighborhood and community level, The Democracy Collaborative has launched multiple programs, platforms, and networks to catalyze larger-scale shifts toward a democratic economy that creates broad well-being. The Next System Project, launched with the support of more than 300 leading scholars and activists, is building a comprehensive platform to promote systemic solutions for an age of systemic crisis. Fifty by Fifty, launched by a network of players in employee ownership, is working to catalyze 50 million employee owners by 2050; the project is strategic advisor to the Fund for Employee Ownership at Evergreen. The Healthcare Anchor Network is convening the nation's leading hospitals and health systems to advance the anchor mission of healthcare across the sector. The Democracy Collaborative also consults on the ground in communities, helping local leaders in places like Albuquerque, Miami, Atlanta, and Washington, DC, work together to build wealth that stays local and is broadly shared.

Connect with The Democracy Collaborative at democracycollaborative.org.

Berrett–Koehler Publishers

Berrett-Koehler is an independent publisher dedicated to an ambitious mission: *Connecting people and ideas to create a world that works for all.*

Our publications span many formats, including print, digital, audio, and video. We also offer online resources, training, and gatherings. And we will continue expanding our products and services to advance our mission.

We believe that the solutions to the world's problems will come from all of us, working at all levels: in our society, in our organizations, and in our own lives. Our publications and resources offer pathways to creating a more just, equitable, and sustainable society. They help people make their organizations more humane, democratic, diverse, and effective (and we don't think there's any contradiction there). And they guide people in creating positive change in their own lives and aligning their personal practices with their aspirations for a better world.

And we strive to practice what we preach through what we call "The BK Way." At the core of this approach is *stewardship,* a deep sense of responsibility to administer the company for the benefit of all of our stakeholder groups, including authors, customers, employees, investors, service providers, sales partners, and the communities and environment around us. Everything we do is built around stewardship and our other core values of *quality, partnership, inclusion,* and *sustainability.*

This is why Berrett-Koehler is the first book publishing company to be both a B Corporation (a rigorous certification) and a benefit corporation (a for-profit legal status), which together require us to adhere to the highest standards for corporate, social, and environmental performance. And it is why we have instituted many pioneering practices (which you can learn about at www.bkconnection.com), including the Berrett-Koehler Constitution, the Bill of Rights and Responsibilities for BK Authors, and our unique Author Days.

We are grateful to our readers, authors, and other friends who are supporting our mission. We ask you to share with us examples of how BK publications and resources are making a difference in your lives, organizations, and communities at www.bkconnection.com/impact.

Dear reader,

Thank you for picking up this book and welcome to the worldwide BK community! You're joining a special group of people who have come together to create positive change in their lives, organizations, and communities.

What's BK all about?

Our mission is to connect people and ideas to create a world that works for all.

Why? Our communities, organizations, and lives get bogged down by old paradigms of self-interest, exclusion, hierarchy, and privilege. But we believe that can change. That's why we seek the leading experts on these challenges—and share their actionable ideas with you.

A welcome gift

To help you get started, we'd like to offer you a **free copy** of one of our bestselling ebooks:

www.bkconnection.com/welcome

When you claim your **free ebook**, you'll also be subscribed to our blog.

Our freshest insights

Access the best new tools and ideas for leaders at all levels on our blog at ideas.bkconnection.com.

Sincerely,

Your friends at Berrett-Koehler